CW01080742

PACK YOUR OWN
HEALTHCARE PARACHUTE

A Physician's Death
Through His Daughter's Eyes

Shiella Dowlatshahi

PACK YOUR OWN HEALTHCARE PARACHUTE:
A Physician's Death Through His Daughter's Eyes
www.HealthcareParachute.com

Copyright © 2023 Shiella Dowlatshahi

Paperback ISBN: 979-8-3735-3441-3

All rights reserved. No portion of this book may be reproduced mechanically, electronically, or by any other means, including photocopying, without permission of the publisher or author except in the case of brief quotations embodied in critical articles and reviews. It is illegal to copy this book, post it to a website, or distribute it by any other means without permission from the publisher or author.

References to internet websites (URLs) were accurate at the time of writing. Authors and the publishers are not responsible for URLs that may have expired or changed since the manuscript was prepared.

Limits of Liability and Disclaimer of Warranty
The author and publisher shall not be liable for your misuse of the enclosed material. This book is strictly for informational and educational purposes only.

Warning – Disclaimer
The purpose of this book is to educate and entertain. The author and/or publisher do not guarantee that anyone following these techniques, suggestions, tips, ideas, or strategies will become successful. The author and/or publisher shall have neither liability nor responsibility to anyone with respect to any loss or damage caused, or alleged to be caused, directly or indirectly by the information contained in this book.

Medical Disclaimer
The medical or health information in this book is provided as an information resource only, and is not to be used or relied on for any diagnostic or treatment purposes. This information is not intended to be patient education, does not create any patient-physician relationship, and should not be used as a substitute for professional diagnosis and treatment.

Publisher
10-10-10 Publishing
Markham, ON Canada

Printed in Canada and the United States of America

For My Father,
Bahram Dowlatshahi, MD.

Contents

Acknowledgments

In this book, I have opened my heart and soul, sharing many of the vulnerabilities during an exceedingly challenging time. Two forces constantly collided, one representing hope and the other a bitter reality that faced our family. My sister represented hope, while I prepared to face my father's mortal life, a beautiful life indeed, coming to an end. The tragedy of my father's sudden illness hit like a cyclone, destroying the centrifugal force that kept us together as a family. Friction within our family was compounded by the realities of a broken healthcare system, designed for profit instead of patients. Witnessing the barriers physicians and staff faced made it difficult to hold anyone accountable. Mortality is ever-present yet ending our lives with dignity is seldom a matter of consideration. Our journey of life begins at birth, vigorously celebrated—can death be viewed as a celebration of a beautiful life?

I know that rehashing some of the past events will be difficult for many to read, including my own two sisters and my mom. The purpose of the book is not to blame or revisit the events but to help families out there facing similar situations. My hope is for those families with terminally ill loved ones to find peace and focus on the celebration of the life of their loved ones rather than their death. I am eternally indebted to friends and family who kept me going during this harrowing time. The list of the people I need to thank for support throughout my father's illness is too long to write out, and I would invariably end up leaving someone out. Nonetheless, I will do my best to acknowledge the many people who inspired me to continue to write what began as a cathartic and therapeutic activity of capturing the pain and suffering as it was happening and sharing the details of my experience with only the keyboard of my computer.

The first of the lengthy list is my mother, Shayesteh Dowlatshahi, who rose to the occasion and embodied selfless love throughout my father's illness. While trying to reconcile how she would ever live without my father, she carried on her role as his wife and cared for him while ignoring her own basic needs, like food and sleep. She courageously took charge to allow my father's wishes to be carried out. Her bravery and stamina amaze me to this day. I know my father is smiling down on her from heaven, thanking her every day for how she loved and cared for him.

My sisters and I began the journey as one unit. At some point, we broke off like the branches of a tree in a windstorm. The storm separated us, leaving our relationship strained to this day. I extend my apologies to both of my sisters; we were all trying to do what we thought was the best for Dad as we went through the grieving process ourselves. I know Dad is still looking down on us girls, hoping we resolve our differences and unite to support each other and our mom.

To my professors, Daniel Carr, Ylisabyth Bradshaw, and Pam Ressler, I am forever indebted to you for your kindness, compassion, and understanding. You were my crutches when I struggled to walk. You made certain I did not succumb to despair while caring for my father. Your guidance gave me the strength to continue the program and graduate.

With heartfelt appreciation and love to my dear friends and neighbors, I am forever thankful to all who have supported me throughout my entire adult life. There are too many to list, and you know who you are. And to all the doctors, nurses, and pharmacists whom I have come to know and befriend over the years, you have been a source of knowledge, inspiration, and enthusiastic support for this book. Your friendship has meant the world to me. I especially thank David Liu for offering exceptional insight as I wrote chapters 8 and 9.

Thank you to the New England Crohn's and Colitis Foundation staff, led by Jenna Wilson, board members, and volunteers. Volunteering with you all has given me the opportunity to redirect the stress and anxiety about my child's well-being into creative energy and passion for carrying on the mission to find a cure so no child or adult will have to experience these horrific diseases. The inflammatory bowel disease physician community is among the most brilliant group of doctors I have come to know. I commend you all for what you do every day. As I often say, this community has been like a second family, supporting me personally through the years.

To those I have had the privilege to work with over the years, I am grateful for the understanding and support I received during my father's illness. Thank you to Mike Bolinder, Jim DiPofi, and Gabriel Fox, who offered their support while I was grieving the loss of my beloved father.

I extend my deepest gratitude to Raymond Aaron, *the New York Times* best-selling author, who enabled this dream to become a reality, and to my editors, including Tracy Knepple, who hung in there with me throughout the process of authoring this book.

Last and most important are my two adult children, Daniel and Alexandra, whom I love and adore. They have been there with me every step of the way through the difficulties of my personal life, supporting me and giving me the latitude to be myself. I never thought they would be the ones who would someday hold me in their arms as I grieved the loss of my father. They have been my rock throughout this journey, and I cannot imagine my world without them. Indeed, I am a proud momma and love them more than life itself.

Foreword

When a close member of your family is faced with news of a terminal diagnosis, shock and denial are your typical reactions. In *Pack Your Own Healthcare Parachute: A Physician's Death Through His Daughter's Eyes*, Shiella Dowlatshahi opens up about her father's cancer diagnosis, and how this news impacted her family dynamic forever. She shares lessons she learned that might help your family during a health crisis.

Shiella begins by introducing her close-knit immigrant family and describing the circumstances that prevented their return to Iran after her father completed his medical training in cardiology. Forced out of their home country, they lost everything and started over in the U.S., facing the daily challenges of assimilating to a new culture. Dr. Dowlatshahi began his career anew, emerging as one of the best doctors in the community. Yet, nothing would prepare this family for the ultimate juxtaposition of the doctor becoming the patient. A rare cancer diagnosis shook their world, eventually dividing the family as they encountered extraordinarily complex decisions along this arduous journey.

As Shiella recounts her family's heartbreaking journey, she shares important knowledge to help you navigate the evolving healthcare system. The current system makes it difficult for providers to advocate for their patients. Shiella writes about how you should be a well-educated healthcare consumer, staying vigilant to ensure your loved ones receive the best care possible.

Additionally, Shiella refers to cultural diversity and how ethnic dissimilarities can affect your family's response to life-changing news. She also shares salient advice on balancing quality of life with the extension of life when a loved one is diagnosed with a terminal illness. Adding to the complexities of your family's response to this life-altering news is how you grieve, making it more onerous to reach a consensus about critical health decisions.

The presence of compassion, patience, and empathy among your family members is crucial in preventing discord. *Pack Your Own Healthcare Parachute: A Physician's Death Through His Daughter's Eyes* is the story of one family's journey of love, loss, and lessons learned along the way, a guide to help your family in your struggle with a loved one's terminal illness.

Raymond Aaron
***New York Times* Bestselling Author**

Chapter 1

One Precious Life

Thursday, March 12th

I opened my eyes after what felt like just a few moments of sleep, to see him lying motionless in the bed across the room. A light tint of yellow on his skin had replaced his usually glowing olive skin. Short gray stubble covered his face now, aging him even more. Surveying his eyelids for a few minutes, I grew more despondent with the lack of movement. In the silence of the room, his shallow breaths were marked. One look at the monitor told me all I needed to know. His mouth was still open; I could almost fool myself into thinking he was in a deep sleep, taking a break from a long snore. He was cold to the touch and did not react as he had in the past few weeks when I squeezed his hand.

Tears started to collect in my eyes, and before I knew it, they were racing down my face. Why him? Why now? He had so much to do on this Earth. None of it made sense to me. As I gathered the thin, hospital-issued blanket, frequently used as my pillow and cover, I popped the reclining chair back into position. The leg rest snapped back, making a loud noise. I looked to see if he heard anything, hoping he would open his eyes or move—just one more time. Startled by the gentle whisper, my attention turned to Mom. She spoke up softly from the couch just next to his bed. "Is everything OK?" I walked over to her, resting my hand on her shoulder, and whispered, "Yes, no change since last night." I noticed the barely audible piano music was still playing on my phone. Classical music and piano solos were supposed to be calming. So, I faithfully played the music, hoping it would be a source of peace and tranquility in the room. Walking slowly toward his bed, I took his hand in mine and caressed it with a squeeze to let him know I was right next to him. "I love you, Daddy." How would I even begin to pray for my father, and what would I pray for? I began to recite prayers about life, love, and saying goodbye when I was not reading poems by Rumi, Dad's favorite poet. It was just Mom and me this morning. Somehow it was peaceful despite what we were facing.

We both knew things were not looking good. It was an unspoken understanding between us. Sleep deprivation had set in after spending three nights at the hospital. But when I thought about how my mother had been at my dad's side for the last seven months, night and day, in and out of the hospital, I knew there was no room for my fatigue. Perhaps a quick refresh would help. I washed my face and brushed my teeth in the sterile-looking bathroom. After a rapid change of clothes, I ran out to be sure I did not miss a single second of being near Dad. Moving to his side, I placed the oral swab into the small plastic cup, wetting it enough to blot Dad's lips. Sometimes he would close his mouth when the sponge rubbed against his teeth. But not today. He remained still. Not a single movement. Could I hope and pray for a miracle now? Miracles happen; maybe if I prayed enough, he would open his eyes and begin to smile. Oh, I wanted that more than anything I have ever wanted in my life. "God, can't we please talk about this? Do you have to take him from us now? I just want him to be OK. He's not ready to leave us. Please, God." My tears kept coming as I silently pleaded. There was nothing that would make them go away today.

"Would you like him to get his antibiotics today?" I simply shook my head to confirm we wanted the antibiotics to continue. The nurse whispered with a gentle smile, startling me as he walked in to check my father's vital signs. He was one of the nurses on the oncology floor. I was unsure which I was drawn to more, his piercing blue eyes or his kind and caring approach each time we needed to make a decision. He straightened Dad's blankets and fluffed the pillow a little under Dad's head. Then he took Dad's hand, felt his pulse, and began counting his breaths, staring at the round clock on the wall just above the whiteboard hanging in front of the bed. Something was different about the whiteboard. The only writing on the board today was the nurse and tech's name and the date. Nothing was written on the board under "goals for today" or "questions for the doctors." Nothing to indicate that a change was possible. The whiteboard seemed to suggest there was no miracle on the way.

The nurse looked at me when he noticed that I had been staring at the board. He did not have to say a word. His eyes were telling me the situation was grim. "His heart rate is very high. I can get him just a little more Dilaudid to make his breathing less labored. Would you like me to do that?" I think I muttered, "Yes, please do." I tried to answer his questions, but my thoughts were racing between what I hoped for and the reality I was facing. But above all else, I just wanted Dad to be comfortable.

We had agreed to continue the antibiotics to prevent his jaundice from appearing. It was strictly a comfort measure for the family, that is. The previous evening, we stopped having him poked with needles in the middle of the night. They had also stopped checking his blood glucose every few hours. No more insulin to poke through his skin, and no more blood thinners injected. He had had enough of all of it. It would be nice not to poke him with needles for at least a day or two. The skin on his legs was starting to look purplish, matching his many bruises from all the needles. His urine was turning an amber color, and there was hardly any of it in the clear bag that rested against the bed. Fluid around his ankles had subsided a little, but his toes still looked swollen. I picked up a washcloth, gently rubbing it on his head to freshen him up. I went over his eyes softly and wiped the rest of his face—anything to stimulate movement. The round table, now holding lab reports we used to have the staff

3

print for us daily caught my eye. No reports were printed this morning. My thoughts were interrupted again when I noticed my mom had left and was returning to the room.

She handed me a fresh cup of coffee. I gulped, confirming it was the same bad coffee I had the day before. Then I thanked Mom for bringing me caffeine to help me through the day. "How did we get to this point?" I thought about the question still haunting me.

I started to replay the tape in my head. Everything happened so quickly, yet it had been seven long months. I was barely speaking with my younger sister and avoiding my older sister altogether. Instead of coming together, the family had fallen apart. It was just the opposite of what Dad had wished when he was diagnosed. He would have wanted us all to care for each other, be kind to one another, respect each other's opinions, and love each other unconditionally. None of that was the case now. I wondered if Dad had heard the family discussions in the room, ranging from his chemo to a possible secondary diagnosis and brain surgery. We even argued over plant-based food instead of traditional Persian meals just after his diagnosis.

Had he been conscious enough to hear our explosive arguments and the many hurtful exchanges in the last few days? What would Dad have said if he could muster up enough energy? Knowing what he knew now, what did Dad think about the treatment approach and how far he would be willing to go? Between hospitalizations, when he was at home and feeling better, Dad was aware of the unpleasant friction between family members. He asked my sister if she could please forgive and forget whatever had happened between us before his last hospital admission in February. I felt bad for letting things get to this point with my siblings, but the more I tried, the more I sank into the quagmire of anger and despair, which fed into the negative energy that flowed between us.

Reflection on the events leading up to today interrupted my reading of Rumi. The replay of events started in my head. Precisely seven days prior, my father's condition took a turn for the worse. We had a gastroenterology consult at my sister's request to find out if we may be able to get rid of the many pockets of infection on my father's liver, which was still unresponsive to antibiotics. A few days before the consultation, doctors drained infectious fluid from his abdomen to relieve some of the pressure, which appeared to be one of the sources of Dad's discomfort. I did not realize that the procedure was an additional source of discomfort.

This intervention seemed reasonable at the time. Looking back, that was another unnecessary procedure that only hurt my father. The fluid was sent to the lab to identify the bacteria. That evening, when I returned to my parents' home from the hospital to get some sleep, my mother called me. She was frantic, and it took me a second to understand what she was saying. When she calmed down a bit, she told me that one of the hospitalists came by to ask to speak to the family. Since she did not quite trust her ability to understand all the technical terms, she wanted him to talk to one of us girls.

My older sister had just left town for an important business meeting the next day. She had instructed me to call her only in case of an emergency. It was a Thursday, and she reluctantly let me take her to the airport. My mom did not want to bother my sister since it was late, and she had an early morning the next day.

That is how I ended up taking the call that was a crushing blow to all our hopes. I agreed to speak with the doctor, and Mom put him on the speaker. I listened intently as he nervously delivered the information. Even though his voice was faint, he spoke deliberately, with incredible compassion. But I knew from that shaky start that the news was not good.

I braced myself for what was to come. I took a deep breath to calm the racing thoughts in my head. Sliding down the wall as the conversation continued, I found myself sitting on the floor. My heart skipped a beat, and tears formed in my eyes. I barely heard a word the first time, so I asked him to repeat himself. "What I'm saying is that your father's condition is grave. He has multiple infections. Without antibiotics, he would be expected to live only a few more days. With the antibiotics on board, I don't expect him to live more than a week."

The doctor's words rang in my ears like a bad echo. Breathing through my mouth and taking deep abdominal breaths did not seem to help. My heart was racing as I began to break into a cold sweat. I wanted to speak, but the words would not come to me. By now, I had given up trying to hold back my tears. With my voice cracking and quivering as I tried to speak, I mumbled a few words, asking if they could continue his medications until I had a chance to talk to my sisters and my mom the following day. "Of course, and please feel free to call me tomorrow if I can answer any other questions," was the response I thought I heard in my semi-conscious state. Mom got back on the phone. She had hung on to every word and knew my dad's life was hanging by a thread.

Glancing back to Rumi's poem, I tried to remain in the present. The readings gave me some temporary peace since I knew if Dad could hear, he would be enjoying it.

"Give us good in the house of our present world,
And give us good in the house of our next world.
Make our path pleasant as a garden..."

Thinking about what followed that phone call broke my concentration again as I tried to return to the next verse of the poem. My nerves were shot after the call, and I was in no mood to talk to anyone, especially my older sister.

Yet, the obligation to call her and let her know what had transpired with the doctor drove me to dial her cell, knowing she would not welcome my call. It was 6:00 a.m. when I placed that call. Unfortunately, early morning calls from me only meant I was delivering bad news. She answered with a cold and uninviting hello. Getting right to the point, I told her I thought she should return as soon as possible because Dad's condition had deteriorated. Her response was not surprising or unexpected. A nearly unrecognizable monotone voice responded with, "Nothing changes. All meds will be continued." Trying to be compassionate, I replied, "That is what I have requested." She continued with the same tone. "I will be there when I get there. I am not sure why you needed to call me this early in the morning." I hung up, confused by her response.

I quickly realized that she denied every piece of information I relayed about the seriousness of our father's condition because she could not or would not accept his death. It was a battle, and she was unwilling to let death win, not if she was in charge. She had been a CEO, running an entire company, so how dare death oppose her wishes.

Escaping from the reflections over the last few days, weeks, and months was impossible today. The horrible memories of our feud kept creeping back into my thoughts. Even though I tried to fight them with all my strength, they continued to dominate Rumi's poems. Reflections turned into questions. We began the journey together as one family unit. What went wrong? Could I have been more understanding and compassionate with my sister? Could my actions have contributed to the existing friction and vitriol today?

After the interaction with my sister that fateful morning, I knew it was time to turn to the only one who may be able to help. I had walked to the church inside the hospital, not knowing why or for what I would be praying. The only thing I knew was I was not praying for a miracle. It was too late for that. During the last seven months, we all prayed for a miraculous cure. My father had

7

fought bravely. During the last several weeks, he had put his dignity aside and accepted being utterly reliant on the oncology floor nurses and medical assistants around him, who approached with kindness and a warm smile. It was as if they were trying to say, "It is OK. We understand this is not easy for you, and we are here to help you. We got this!"

Tears began to run down my face in the small, quiet church that suddenly became larger with the presence of a life greater than me. My eyes were drawn to the ceiling, where a bright light shone down in my direction, but there was no actual ceiling chandelier or light. Instead, this bright light became increasingly apparent as I stared up. Suddenly, I knew what to say. It was all crystal clear now.

I prayed to God in that small hospital church to give Dad peace. "Please, God, if it is time for my father to come to you, take him swiftly. Take him before he endures another day of pain and suffering. No more needles, blood tests, and pumping him with fluids only to make him more uncomfortable. I beg you to take him now if it is the right time. Let me be by his side to hold his hand through his journey to you. I beg you to let me be there to give him a last kiss goodbye and let him know that he will always be alive in my heart."

There was still no one around me. My tears had turned to quiet sobs as I reached for the Kleenex box on top of the church pews—as if that box would be enough to dry up the river running down my face. Even as the crying continued, I felt a warm wave come over my entire body as though an angel was embracing me. It was as though someone else was taking a deep breath for me. For the first time in seven months, I was calm. I was confident that no matter what came my way from my sister, I was determined not to let her order more tests, procedures, or medications. I wanted to spend every moment with my father, at his side, praying with him, and making sure that he knew he would not be alone for even one moment going forward.

My sister arrived later that day, anger competing with her pain, denial competing with acceptance, and suffering competing with the tranquility of letting go. Uneasiness grew more palpable as I saw her struggling to accept the present. Indeed, suffering ends when we accept the present and let go of the past. Yet, accepting the "now" is admitting to the reality before us, something she was not ready to do.

"Do not go gentle into that good night." Who knew Dylan Thomas's poetry could accurately describe my culture and family? The basic human instinct is to hold onto life and fight for it. Persian culture denies death to the very end. There is always one more thing to do or try. Putting up a fight means denying the end and refusing to give in to the inevitable. If you do not discuss death among family or friends, it does not exist and cannot hurt you.

Sadly, Mom and Dad rarely discussed the topic regarding their own lives. During his final hospitalization, when he was alone with my mom, he suddenly looked at her and said, "I think I'm going to leave this world soon." He had decided it was time, and no procedure or test would change that. Was he looking for her to allow him to go? I do not know, because he did not say a word after this declaration. He knew. And she knew.

"Goodbyes are only for those who love with their eyes. Because for those who love with heart and soul, there is no such thing as separation."

I finished the Rumi poem and gently laid my head on Dad's arm, asking God for comfort and peace for my dad, and the wisdom and strength to handle what we were about to face as a family. Tears stung my face as they raced onto my Dad's still arm. Memories of the past flickered in my head as I closed my eyes for a momentary reprieve from my aching heart.

Chapter 2

Dad's Early Days

My father was proud of his heritage and the Dowlatshahi name. He often enlightened us about Iran's history, the great Persian Empire, and his lineage. The Qajar dynasty was the Iranian monarchy that ruled Persia from 1785–1925, and was succeeded by the Pahlavi dynasty, Iran's last monarchy. Mohammad Ali Mirza Dowlatshah was a Persian prince of the Qajar dynasty, and the progenitor of the family name Dowlatshahi of Persia. He ruled at the astonishingly young age of nine as the governor of Fars and became ruler in the city of Kermanshah at age 19 by defeating the Russians, their archrivals. He established the city of Dowlat-Abad, later renamed Malayer. Dowlatshah's ten sons had children of their own, and his descendants now live all over the world and carry the name Dowlatshahi (English Spelling), which means "of the Dowlatshah empire." With that history lesson came a lot of pride in the Persian culture and Dad's insistence that we learn as much as possible about Persian history, architecture, and art.

Although his lineage was royalty, my father never spoke of growing up as one. My grandfather was an intelligent and successful businessman in Iran, with an incredible sense of humor. I had the pleasure of being around him for a part of my life, and I still recall his intense interest in world news and his love of family and friends. When my father's mom passed away from complications of diabetes and heart disease, Dad decided to pursue a life in the medical field. He was nineteen at the time and had no idea how his father would be able to afford medical school for him and his brother. Two of the three boys in the family were accepted into the prestigious Tehran University of Medical Sciences.

To ease the burden on the family finances, my father decided to join the army, fully funding his education through his military service. He quickly became known in his peer group as the genius everyone wanted to sit next to in class. Always prepared and ready to answer questions, he was known as the hard-working, conscientious brother. Dad's goal at the time was to speak fluent English, not only for casual conversation but also to translate medical terms. Visits to the library to study and perfect his English became a part of Dad's routine in medical school. Meanwhile, his younger brother seemed to have different goals.

My uncle had an uncanny resemblance to my father, and he enjoyed socializing more than studying. My father spoke fondly of the times when his brother got in trouble in school and was called into the provost's office. Of course, my father would defend his brother, often getting him out of trouble for violation of curfews and missing class. Dad had a way of communicating that rendered others defenseless immediately. Later, my uncle would hear about his indiscretions from his brother in private. His timely humor, kindness, and humility were a salve during difficult conversations.

After completing medical school at the top of his class, the new graduate was granted a residency in the United States of America. A dream for many became reality for my father quickly after graduation. Surprised and enthusiastic about his journey and his next few years in America, he soon realized he wanted to begin his next chapter as a married man. Going to his uncle for help with choosing his forever partner was the logical next step. The search soon began, with his uncle taking the driver seat, literally, as they went shopping for the perfect woman to marry.

Dad loved to tell the story about how he and my mom met. A smile would immediately appear on his face, and his eyes would light up as he relived the day that he met Mom. Tears of joy would run down his face as he transported us all back to that magical day. Then he would finish reciting a poem from Rumi about the beauty of life.

"When I run after what I think I want,
my days are a furnace of distress and anxiety;
if I sit in my own place of patience,
what I need flows to me, and without any pain.
From this, I understand that what I want also wants me,
and is looking for me and attracting me.
There's a great secret in this for all who can grasp it."

Of course, as traditions go, their marriage was arranged, though neither bride nor groom were forced into it. Generations of testimonials defend the concept of arranged marriages and why they work in countries like Iran. During my father's era, it was customary for elder family members to act as matchmakers. They would select the bride for an eligible bachelor, considering many factors, such as religious background, socioeconomic class, and education. Dad and his uncle set out to visit 10 families with daughters eligible for marriage. As I understand it, families went through a significant amount of preparation prior to this type of visit, making sure everything was perfect for the meeting with the potential groom. The family would spend nearly the entire visit with the potential groom and his family members. The eligible bachelorette would only appear in the room during the final minutes, either clearing the tea away or offering more sweets, giving the bachelor just a few minutes to get a good look at his potential future wife. The process emphasized the importance of alignment between the two families over anything else.

According to Dad, couples rarely saw each other before the planned marriage, yet they began to fall in love as soon as they consented to wed their new partner. As for Dad, his visits to the nine families went well, but none of the bachelorettes impressed him. Dad would tell us how he took one look at my mom when she entered the room and instantly knew. She was the tenth woman and the final family they visited.

"She is the one. I think I'm in love. I am going to marry her," my father exclaimed after leaving Mom's home with his uncle. His uncle warned him not to make a hasty decision. But Dad was certain he had found the right woman to be his partner. She would be the woman of his dreams, by his side for better or for worse, for the rest of his life. He would cherish her as long as he lived.

My mother enthusiastically welcomed the idea of marrying Dad. I don't know if she realized that her decision to consent to the marriage would dramatically change her life as she knew it. After Dad spent the rest of his savings on Mom's wedding rings, they packed up and headed to the United States for their extended honeymoon and Dad's next three years of internal medicine residency.

Mom did not speak any English and was not aware of how difficult medical residency would be for Dad. Residency required him to spend most of his waking hours at the hospital, often working for thirty-six hours at a time. Indeed, residency was not easy for my father, yet he never discussed how difficult things were. Instead, he focused on moments of peace and the little things that brought him contentment. My father's face lit up when he talked about how he looked forward to returning to the dingy old apartment near the hospital during a rare break to spend a few minutes with Mom. He would laugh as he told us about the time he caught Mom cleaning baseboards with a toothbrush or painting a room a more pleasant color. As soon as Dad arrived, Mom would drop everything, eagerly greeting him before serving freshly prepared rice and a Persian stew of meat and vegetables. Instead of enjoying their meal together, too often, his beeper would go off. Soon he would be back in the hospital, leaving Mom with a house full of chores. Even on the days he was home, if he was on call, plans could be disrupted at a moment's notice if he was needed at the hospital. Still, those days were extremely exciting for Mom and Dad.

Blessed with two babies over those three years, my mother was incredibly busy, learning a new language and customs while managing motherhood without her own mother and extended family. After Dad completed his residency in internal medicine, it was time to return to Iran. It had been a long three years for them. They were newlyweds in a foreign country, learning to assimilate. Yet, they were grateful for the memories of their time in the United States with each other, friends, and their newborns. Dad would often look up to the sky, thanking God and exclaiming my sister and I were their most prized additions to their lives, adding to the joy and juggling that defines parenthood during the baby and toddler years.

Things did not get less challenging when they returned to Iran. My older sister and I spoke English before we learned how to speak Farsi, the Persian language. When we returned to Iran as toddlers, my grandmother struggled to communicate with both of us. She spoke Persian and fluent Russian, but neither language helped her. Instead of speaking, she would make facial expressions to relay her feelings of excitement before she learned a few words in English to communicate better with her grandchildren. Our youngest sister was born in Iran shortly after we moved back. As I see it, a father of three or more daughters should be designated a title of sainthood. A four-woman household meant lots of opinions and plenty of requests. It was not easy to satisfy all of us girls, but Dad worked hard at it. Our happiness was everything to our dear father.

When we were younger, Mom used to dress us in our fancy dresses and tights to go out after Dad was finished with his patients on Friday evenings. Exhausted from seeing fifty-plus patients, he would eagerly change his clothes and smile at my mom, expressing his enthusiasm for our outing. We would be fighting with our tights, frustrated about why we had to endure such uncomfortable contraptions. He would come over to us, gently pick us up by the tights, and swing us around until they were perfectly pulled up. "All set!" he would exclaim before moving on to the next unhappy little girl. We would laugh and giggle, enjoying the little ride, quickly forgetting about all our fights with the tights—problem solved with a little patience and a lot of laughter.

When it came to medical issues, we always sought Dad's advice. One night, my younger sister, five or six years old at the time, woke up and headed to my parents' room because she felt unwell. Before leaving our room, she woke me up. As her older sister, I wanted to help and climbed the countertops to find some stomach medications I had seen my dad grab for himself. Good thing Dad heard all the noise as the bottles of medicine hit the counter and the floor one by one. Although he never raised his voice, Dad made it clear that I should never grab any medications or try to treat my sister. But he did thank me for being a concerned and caring older sister. Off to the hospital they went after my father quickly examined my sister, determining appendicitis was a likely diagnosis. My sister was quickly rushed to the operating room for surgery to remove her appendix. The incident ended my short-lived career as a diagnostician or healer. I continued to try to diagnose and treat but kept my practice limited to my dolls after that incident.

As a newly promoted officer and a practicing physician, Dad's responsibilities with the Shah's army grew. He had worked hard for seven or eight straight years after returning to Iran. Climbing the ladder and achieving the rank of a colonel was not what Dad discussed as the highlight of his career, even though his high rank as an army officer provided him with privileges and comforts of life rarely afforded to others outside of the Pahlavi Monarchy. Protection was provided for a colonel's family around the clock, with army soldiers assigned to the house of each officer. We also enjoyed the services of a full-time housekeeper. For that, we traded time with Dad as he was called out at all hours of the day and night, fulfilling his duties in the army and private practice responsibilities.

We had the opportunity to attend Persian American schools while living in Iran. At one point, we were taught by nuns at Soheil School. The school consisted of a half Persian and half English curriculum. Swim club and sports events filled our summer days and evenings. One of my fondest memories was attending the professional soccer games where my father would tend to the players as their physician.

The swim club introduced us to iconic all-American foods, such as hamburgers, hot dogs, and French fries, as well as teaching us how to swim. We looked forward to swimming lessons and showing off what we had learned when our father joined us on weekends. We would jump into the pool, with my mom carefully watching just outside the pool. Heated pools did not exist. I recall all three of us girls being so cold that our lips would turn purple, and our toes would go numb. We ignored our slight unease in the freezing water in exchange for the fun we had. My father would already be in the shallow end, encouraging us, in turn, to jump in and swim to him. When we got closer, he would move back just a few inches to have us swim farther. Soon, we were on to him and objected fiercely. However, he would simply give us his encouraging smile and tell us how proud he was. That was all we needed to hear to keep going. My father was so intuitive regarding when to use humor, and encouraged us to keep moving forward, especially when we just wanted to quit.

With Dad's encouragement, I even entered a swimming competition at the club. I came in fifth place, and I was so proud of myself because of all the accolades Dad gave me. When we got to our cousin's house that evening, I proudly told everyone how I had come in fifth place in the swim meet, receiving congratulations from everyone. Finally, one of my older cousins asked how many participants were in the competition. "There were six kids swimming," I exclaimed proudly. As an eight-year-old, it never occurred to me that there was anything wrong with where I had placed. The number of kids competing did not matter to my father. He was proud of me because I got out of my comfort zone. Although we did not all get a medal, I was proud to have been a participant. This was my first entry into competing, something I found enjoyable and rewarding growing up.

One of the traditions I missed most when we left Iran was the celebration of Chaharshanbe Suri and Nowruz with extended family. The last Wednesday of the year was celebrated vigorously by Iranians, in what was called the Festival of Fire. After a long winter indoors, families looked forward to this outing just before the coming of the first day of spring, known as Nowruz or the Persian New Year. Families come together around bonfires and lights to celebrate the end of the year and usher in the Persian New Year, wishing health and happiness for all. Children would line up in their yards, singing songs and jumping over small fire-lit bushes to cleanse themselves of any evils of the year. The act of jumping over the fire was the symbolic crossing over from sickness to health and asking for the redness and the purity of fire to remove any illness or impurities.

In anticipation of the celebration, wheat or lentil grass is grown to set the traditional table with seven items beginning with the letter "S" in Persian language. Large mirrors, decorated eggs, and elaborate floral arrangements covered Haftsin tables for the largest celebration of the year. Other items included dried fruits, candles, vinegar, coins, and garlic. Each item represented something unique, having to do with health, longevity, abundance, and protection from illness and evil. Homes would get a new facelift, sparkling clean, awaiting company. Families visited each other in their brand-new clothes throughout the holiday, sharing meals and sweets and wishing each other health and happiness. Time with family and friends was the focus during this celebration, which lasted almost two weeks. On the thirteenth day, there were picnics outdoors with music, dancing, and audible laughter everywhere as families got rid of the grown wheatgrass in the nearby waters.

For vacations, we would head to the beautiful waters of the Caspian Sea, a true retreat for our family. There, we would spend the summers at our newly built villa. Dad bought the land years before building a villa there. The villa was not extravagant, but it was our special retreat. I still remember the beautifully placed round windows in each room, looking out to sea. My uncles and grandmother would often accompany us on our vacations. After spending the day jumping over the waves and building sandcastles, we spent the night playing cards and backgammon. Mom would make sure everyone stayed close to shore, and she held our towels out when we were done swimming. She was terrified of the water and watched over us carefully, knowing she could not stop us from experiencing the beaches.

Discipline of the girls was relinquished to Mom as we were growing up. There were a few exceptions when she had to threaten us by telling Dad about our misbehavior. We knew if Dad got upset with us, he would give us that look of disappointment that made us want to melt into the crevasses beneath the ground and disappear. Dad never had to raise his voice or his hand. We knew we had disappointed, and that was enough of a punishment. Since no one wanted to endure his disappointment, it was usually enough to get us to behave for Mom.

Planning trips and adventures were Dad's passion, and he never failed to impress us with his grand plans. A few years before destiny had us packing up for what we thought to be a short stint back in the U.S., Dad produced an adventurous vacation idea for the family. One day, he came home beaming with excitement. At dinner, he informed us of the elaborate plan for our summer vacation. My eyes were wide open, staring at the maps he was sharing with us and listening to every word, thinking I was dreaming. Hundreds of questions ran around in my head after pinching myself and realizing that the plan was real. Fly to Germany and meet up with my youngest uncle? So far, all is good. Then visit the BMW factory and hand pick our canary yellow 5 series BMW to purchase? It all sounded great. The next part of the plan had us staring at Dad with wide eyes and smiles, not understanding what it was that we were about to embark on. We would not only purchase our new car in Germany, but we would also take it for a joy ride over the English Channel to England.

After our visit there, we would return and continue our drive all the way to Iran over the next month. It is hard to imagine now that we accomplished this without MapQuest, Waze app, or cell phones. Throughout the month, we drove thousands of kilometers and saw multiple countries, enjoying the unique cuisine of that country and making lots of friends along the way. Our cargo grew as Mom carefully selected the most unique and beautiful pieces of art or décor as a souvenir from each country we visited to bring back home. My sisters and I would lay on top of the growing luggage in the back seat, often joking around about just how high the suitcases underneath us would get by the time we got to our destination. There were no seatbelts in the back seats that I recall at the time. Our little plush back seat had a small mattress that laid on top of the luggage. It was a comfortable way to travel.

We had some near misses during our travels. The most unforgettable was the night we arrived in England after a long and rocky boat ride on a ship large enough to carry our new car. Still nauseous and groggy from the ride, Dad climbed into the driver's seat and began driving. It must have been close to midnight. Suddenly, we woke up to a loud screech and Dad mumbling something about the "truck driver is on the wrong side of the road." It was our brand-new car that was on the wrong side of the road. We owed our lives to the greater power watching over us that night. Dad's sigh of relief told me we were spared any damage. For the rest of our time in England, no one forgot which side of the road we should be driving on, including us girls.

Other than the near miss, the only other incident that still lives with me was driving on the narrow and winding mountainside roads in Turkey, enjoying the beautiful yet terrifying views as we stared at the ravines below us. A battle with another oversized truck would leave us with a beehive-like shattered windshield. Insects accompanied us in the extremely hot car with a missing windshield for the rest of our trip home. At the border of Turkey and Iran, the girls broke out into a rash, later diagnosed to be German measles, our own special souvenir from Europe that summer. Let us say I did not run out of ideas for the school essay about my summer vacation that year.

Like our road trip, life for the Dowlatshahi family was full of adventure, with change as the only constant. We learned to be adaptable, embrace change, and trust that everything did happen for a reason. In 1977, another opportunity presented itself for Dad to specialize further in cardiology. We would pack up and move to Michigan, the state we were born in and the location of Dad's fellowship in cardiology.

When we returned to the U.S. in 1977, we did not know it would be a very tenuous time for us as a family for the next few years. We moved to Michigan with seven suitcases and two Persian rugs, leaving behind our favorite dolls, toys, and family photos locked up in our home. Our plan was to return after two years so that we could finish upper school in Iran prior to returning to the States for college and beyond. Destiny would have a different plan for the Dowlatshahi family.

Chapter 3

Severed from His Country

After we settled back in Michigan, Dad purchased a Chevy Impala, and we moved into a modest townhome, which would be our temporary digs. We were excited about the wall-to-wall carpeting. All we had ever seen in Iran were Persian rugs covering the floors. We were thrilled with simple new experiences like taking a bus to school and using the vacuum cleaner.

America represented the hope of endless achievements without limitations to any level of success as a female. Of course, many may believe that the land of the free and the proud still has its own set of issues. In general terms, many who have come to this country to become citizens have done so because they have more faith in their life's dreams coming true in this country versus their home country. We knew that achieving our dreams as females in Iran was near impossible. Excited about the notion of life in the U.S. as adults, we looked forward to excelling in the English language, learning more about American people and their traditions, and fully assimilating. In exchange, we would offer our classmates information about our backgrounds, our rich Persian culture, and the heritage that made us proud of the Dowlatshahi name. We brought the best of our homeland to our new country, but that did not mean others were interested in what we had to offer. What we did not know was that we were going to face incredible challenges in settling into our new home.

For bonuses go to ...

As we began attending school as teenagers in a different country, our differences became apparent. We were sporting our thick accents, despite being fluent in English. We wore European clothes. As a teenager, blending in with your peers is important. We were soon known as the Dowlatshahi girls from a foreign country; we stuck out like sore thumbs. We enjoyed riding a bus to school until the bullying got to be difficult to ignore. We learned to keep to ourselves and traveled together on and off the bus. I recall being brutally bullied and punched by a girl once as I got off the bus. I never even knew the girl or talked to her before she attacked me. Because I was Persian and different, she took it upon herself to let me know she did not approve of my presence. Diversity was not a topic anyone cared about in the late 1970s.

Unfamiliar with bullying, we had a cruel introduction to it during our first year in school in the U.S. We dealt with being made fun of for all our differences in our own ways. My older sister excelled in school and grew in popularity because of her intelligence. I found my passion in sports and began participating in as many of them as I could handle. My younger sister kept to herself, trying to go unnoticed. Losing our European clothes could not happen soon enough; we proudly wore our new Levi jeans, large wool Izod sweaters, and clogs, and quickly assimilated to our new high school environment. Dad worked hard at his fellowship, and Mom was perfect in her support role for the family. But what happened next was one of the most shocking experiences for our family.

"The Shah of Iran has left the country," was the headline on the news on television in 1979, two years after we arrived in the U.S. and only months before we were due to return to the country. The headlines about Iran's revolution filled the world news each night. Horrific pictures accompanied the headlines on the *Iran Times*, a newspaper we were regularly receiving when we first arrived in the U.S. "Death to the Shah; Death to America" were the headlines boldly covering the front page of the *Iran Times* during what came

24

to be known as the Iranian Islamic Revolution. The revolutionaries aimed to remove the monarchy in exchange for establishing an Islamic State and returning to ancient Islamic laws, including cutting off the fingers of women caught on the streets with nail polish, and stoning women to death based on accusations of misbehavior by their husbands.

Tragedy invaded our kitchen table every month with the delivery of the *Iran Times*. Every time I spotted the *Iran Times* on the table, I knew more shocking news was delivered, through pictures of murdered high-ranking officers in the army and their families, many of whom we knew well. Their homes were broken into in the middle of the night. They were lined up and brutally executed. No one was spared, not even the small children. The evidence was in front of us that this would be our destiny if we returned to our home country.

"What is wrong, Daddy?" I recall saying to Dad as I walked through the door to see him sitting at the kitchen table, holding his face in his hands. When he saw me, he quickly wiped his tears with the palms of his hands, pretending all was OK. I knew better. Before he could fold up the paper, I got a glimpse of the headline. His closest friends, physicians, and members of the army were the most recent victims of the revolutionaries. Their bloody photos and names plastered on the paper were all I needed to see to understand the gravity of the situation. There was so much death and destruction. After that night, I noticed frequent calls from those who could get through after hours of trying to dial out of the country to contact my father. These friends and family had either fled the country or were planning to flee. They all had the same advice. "It is not safe for you and your family to return." Dad had a decision to make about our future as a family; to lose what he had worked all his life for, including the homes, land, and our belongings, or return home to face the evils of the new regime. What hurt him the most was facing the dark reality of never seeing his immediate and extended family again. Ultimately, his beloved wife and children were more important to him than anything he would leave behind.

While the Iranian revolution, followed by the hostage takeover at the U.S. embassy that occurred in Iran, are just pages in history now, these events had a profound impact on my family and my teenage years. Memories of friends killed by the revolutionaries are chiseled in my mind. We went from having to acclimate to our environment quickly, knowing that we were going home to Iran in just a couple of years, to realizing that we owned nothing but what we had brought to America in those suitcases and would not be returning anytime soon. Everything else was lost. Because of my father's high rank in the Shah's armed forces, going back to Iran was not a viable option for our family. To return would mean death for my father and our entire family.

My parents chose to stay in America and build a new life. We were severed from our extended family in Iran, and that was the hardest part of all, especially for my parents. "They can take away everything, but they can't take my brain," were the words that I still hear my father saying to the family as he wept and decided to say goodbye to his country, his beloved brothers, and his father, whom he would never see again. What we would do and where we would go were thoughts that kept us awake at night. We had no idea how we would survive in the U.S. Kindness knocked at our door when a retiring physician who knew of my dad's circumstances offered him his practice. Next stop, Rochester, NY.

Chapter 4

Sisterhood

We experienced a lifetime of adventures and adversity during our childhood. These experiences helped build a strong bond between my siblings and me. My older sister and I were so close growing up. Inseparable. Even though college life and our jobs put physical distance between us, we remained besties. The mere two-year difference in our age was never apparent. She was always the more intelligent sister, who prepared her school papers at the last minute and skated through high school and college with A's and A+'s. She was one of seven people at the University of Rochester pursuing a neuroscience degree. Like the rest of us, she was not perfect. My sister was unlikely to take a prize in a competition for the world's neatest person. I remember visiting her in college and asking her how she got in her bed with the multiple layers of clothing covering it. Then she picked up the blanket under her clothes and shook it. We broke into laughter when she successfully landed at least two weeks' worth of clothes on the floor. The two of us laughed a lot and enjoyed each other's company. After college, she immediately began her career in health care, and so did I. We both married and had children of our own.

Surprisingly, as a traditional Persian man with a traditional marriage, Dad always encouraged us to get a college education and be financially independent before choosing love, marriage, and children. Women were to be equals in his mind and deserved the same opportunities afforded to men. We all spent time rotating in Dad's office during summer vacations, rounding with him often at the hospital during the weekends. Making sure we were exposed to a life in medicine was his way of steering us gently, without forcing us into any profession. When we began in our respective jobs, he was always supportive and encouraged us to excel. His eyes lit up with pride when we delivered news of any awards or promotions.

During his rounds, when he was asked about his family and his three girls, he would puff out his chest with pride and let those inquiring know about his daughters' latest achievements. During the early years of our careers, my sister and I worked for competing companies. Dad was always deeply engaged in the discussions about our careers, which often happened during our family gatherings. The debates at the dinner table over our products were settled by Dad acting as our referee. Instead of declaring one of us the winner of the debate, he would choose to recognize the main points of each argument and focus on the similarities of the products instead of the differences. The joke in the family was that my sister went into marketing because of me. I was passionate about my opinions, and she was creative, always coming up with another angle. Together, we were the perfect duo.

Aside from the family discussions at the kitchen table, where he demonstrated how to find peaceful resolutions to our debates, Dad also taught us all how to be in the moment and enjoy every minute with family, especially through our holiday traditions. At Thanksgiving, a holiday Dad particularly enjoyed, the family would gather and spend quality time together during the long weekend. Quite frequently, my sister and I would show up to Thanksgiving dinner with the same exact outfit, purchased from two different cities, without knowing that the other had purchased or would be wearing that outfit. It was evident we were like two peas in a pod, even when we were not around each other daily.

On Black Friday, we would wake up enthusiastically at four in the morning and wait in long lines together, sipping our coffees and buying bags and bags of doorbuster toys for our kids and donations for charity. Late in the afternoon, we would come home exhausted from our outing. By the evening, gifts would be wrapped and ready for our early Christmas celebration with Mom and Dad. My father's greatest delight was having his grandchildren open their presents in the family room. He would capture the precious moments with his Polaroid camera, only to view the pictures multiple times later that weekend, smiling each time he relived their joy.

My father's presence in the room was larger than life. No matter where we were in the house during the Thanksgiving holiday, we would know that my father had returned home from seeing his patients or doing errands. There would be a loud "HALLO" as he entered the house, followed by thunderous footsteps of little ones running to the door to greet him. All the grandchildren competed for time with Papa. One by one, Papa would have them on his lap, telling them stories or making them laugh with his silly jokes. Watching my mom and dad interact with all the kids brought us so much joy.

The grandchildren were mesmerized by Dad. They even tried to emulate his unique way of enjoying breakfast by having orange juice over his cereal when lactose-free milk was unavailable. A banana and peanut butter sandwich became a two-ingredient delicacy using fresh lavash bread from the Middle Eastern market. At dinner, all the kids wanted to sit near Papa. Dad enjoyed his food so much and ate with such fervor that it made everyone around him want to try what he was eating.

Life and work separated us into cities that required a five or six-hour drive to my parents' home. When it came to saying goodbye, we knew Dad would be sad to see us go. Yet, there was always the next holiday or the next family get-together to begin planning. It felt like there would be an eternity of holidays and family gatherings woven into our lives. The memories of these gatherings fed our bonds of love and friendship throughout the rest of the year.

As sisters, we stayed connected about kids, work, and life in general. I was always closer to my older sister and saw her more like a best friend. My younger sister often required more attention by way of counseling and advice about life in general.

My older sister and I agreed on so many things and shared the same philosophy around leadership, management of employees, and standards at the workplace. We were both on leadership tracks early in our careers, except she took the elevator straight up, and I took the steps. There were a few things we differed on. For example, as parents, I was an extremely strict mom, and she was the one every child dreamed their mom to be like. These differences never separated us, and our disagreements never impacted our relationship with one another. We respected each other's opinions and sparred every so often over a controversial topic, laughing and joking as we ended the conversation and moved on to another topic. My sister meant everything to me. She was my confidant and trusted friend. I would share things with her that I would not or could not share with anyone else.

No one could have imagined that a loved one's terminal illness would have separated our family instead of bringing us even closer, especially since we were already so close. In fact, my older sister and I began the journey with my father's illness on the same team—we were TeamDad. Beating cancer was a goal both of us strived to achieve for him. As the cancer rapidly ate away at my father's health and quickly metastasized, it also poisoned our family dynamic, especially the relationship with my older sister. Our differences quickly became the revolting centerpiece of our lives. The venomous words were like a toxin that fed into our negative attitude toward each other.

Our relationship reached the point that we were not able to be in the same room together. Dad's hospital room became a battlefield, where we would begin hurling rebukes at one another, only stopping when interrupted by one of the hospital staff members entering to take vital signs or administer medications. Our sorrow over the situation made it easier to cut each other with our words, creating wounds that do not easily heal. We stopped listening with an open mind and heart. We were opposing forces on the same team, beginning to question and doubt one another on every facet of Dad's care. My mother and younger sister had to delicately dance between us. Neither one wanted to take sides, but both were dealing with their own grief simultaneously.

It was eerily like what was going on in our country with respect to opposing political views. Love of country was shared by all, yet people became discordant, divided, and toxic with vitriol toward one another. It was as though my dad's cancer had impacted the entire country. In fact, the entire world was off and preparing for the calamity that was about to come in the days and months ahead, the pandemic of COVID-19.

Chapter 5

Dealing with a Terminal Diagnosis

Dad had a zest for life, unlike anything I have witnessed, regardless of whether he was at work or spending time with family. Mom had been begging him to slow down and retire for some time. Yet, each time he considered it, he would think about his patients' displeasure when he announced he was going to spend a couple of weeks in Florida during the winter. He felt he was abandoning his patients if he left permanently. "Celebrate each year of life after eighty as a God-given bonus," he would advise his aging patients. He encouraged them to pick up a new hobby, start couple's dance lessons, or pursue a passion after retirement to keep their hearts and minds young.

Quite contrary to his own advice, he claimed work was his hobby and that if he stopped working, his mind would too. Slowly, he began to admit that he should heed his own advice and begin spending less time working and more time relaxing with family. This was not an easy decision for Dad. Although he loved and cherished every moment of his time as a physician, he admitted it was time to step aside a few months prior to his eighty-fifth birthday. When his retirement was announced early in 2019, his mailbox filled up with letters from patients and families thanking him for caring for them. Saying goodbye to his patients was bittersweet; his final days in the office were filled with tears and laughter as he and his staff reminisced about his early days in practice. After he retired, he looked forward to getting together with friends and family, spending time with those who had often had to take a back seat to the realities of a patient-centered physician. As the social planner for the family, my older sister was quick to fill Dad's calendar, including a family reunion to celebrate his upcoming birthday that July.

The lake house was in the Finger Lakes wine region, situated on a few acres of plush green land, facing one of the lakes and large enough to accommodate all of us. It was an older house full of antiques that could tell thousands of stories about the multiple families who had celebrated special occasions there through the years. When my older sister arranged to have my aunt fly out to celebrate his eighty-fifth birthday at the Finger Lakes, Dad was ecstatic. Aunt Hoori was his soulmate growing up. They had the same mannerisms even though they lived on opposite ends of the country and had not seen each other in a decade.

Eager to see his sister, Dad jumped in the car to pick up my Aunt Hoori at the airport with my older sister, despite his fatigue from travel earlier that day. His excitement was infectious. I opted to drive because I did not have any CBD to ingest for the anxiety that came over me with my sister's driving. Not that I was any better. In fact, we all joked around that the Dowlatshahi girls had gone to the Bahram school of driving. Persian music blasted from my car speakers, and we smiled as we listened to our favorite Persian artist, Googoosh, who was exiled from Iran after the revolution. She was the Madonna-like sensation during our time in Iran.

When we arrived at the airport, my dad was the first to spot my aunt. I stayed in the car with my sister as Dad nearly jumped out of the car before we came to a full stop. It was dusk, but I could manage to see my aunt's aging yet still athletic figure in the distance. As soon as they embraced, tears began to roll down their faces. Soon after we saw the two of them, my sister and I looked at each other, knowing the other was also crying. The tears of joy overwhelmed both our faces. The feeling of exultation during our ride back was indescribable. Quickly, we dispatched ourselves from cloud nine and into the house, where Mom had laid out an array of Persian snacks to greet us.

Mom, Aunt Hoori, and Dad soaked up the beautiful sun illuminating the lakefront deck. They took walks every morning, exchanging memories and enjoying each other's company. Dad even managed to hang out with the grandchildren on the beach. He did not love the heat at the beach, but he was not going to miss enjoying time with everyone. It was July and very warm out. Dad became light-headed and needed to sit down for a bit at the beach. Unconcerned, we concluded the incident was a simple case of dehydration. What we did not realize at the time was that a cancerous growth was lurking around, waiting for an opportunity to invade our lives.

Our journey to the horrific diagnosis began only weeks after that family vacation. My younger sister was at my mom and dad's when my father woke up with significant jaundice and itching. Dad was an excellent diagnostician, one of the best. However, he was so obtunded that he could not understand why his skin was yellow or why the whites of his eyes were no longer white and looked pasty with a hint of yellow. After giving it some thought, Dad surmised the jaundice was due to an issue with his liver and the collection of bile that was not being processed as it needed to, resulting in the accumulation of toxic levels in his blood. He called his primary care doctor, who ordered him to have bloodwork done immediately. When his blood test came back highly abnormal, he was promptly sent to the emergency department.

When I heard my dad was admitted with severe jaundice, I traveled to see him in the hospital, from Boston, without a single thought about what our family was about to face. I never expected his jaundice to lead to a terminal diagnosis. This was my father we were talking about. He managed his diabetes and cholesterol impeccably with medications. These medications were his ticket to longevity. Swimming and laughing often were his way of being mindful. He was invincible. So, obviously, the thought of his mortality never entered my mind. I was just not worried about him. Disease of any kind had no chance with my father. He was superhuman.

When I arrived at the hospital, I did not know anything about his potential diagnosis, despite the rumblings of what it might be. Nothing was for certain according to my mom and younger sister, who were at the hospital during Dad's visit to ER and his first hospital admission.

Thankfully, his hospital admission happened to be at the hospital where he had practiced for decades. They recognized him in the emergency room as their favorite internal medicine and cardiology physician. He was affectionately known as "Dr. D" because Dowlatshahi was a tough one to pronounce on the overhead speakers. This became his nickname by default. The emergency room nurses took wonderful care of him, asking about his symptoms and trying to make him comfortable. His discomfort did not impact his sense of humor. When asked, "So, we hear you are one of us. What kind of doctor were you?" Dad quickly replied, "A good one." He loved making others smile with his quick wit. Meanwhile, the ER doctors ordered tests to look more closely at his organs. The news about Dad's test results hit like a cyclone. This was the beginning of some of the darkest times of my life.

After examining the films with the gastroenterologist, a hospitalist just a year out of residency came to see my father alone. He was tearing up, and his lips were quivering as he spoke softly to my mom and dad. The diagnosis was grave. It was cancer, an exceedingly difficult one to treat. According to this young man, five-year survival was grim. Clearly, this inexperienced doctor was the unlucky one having to deliver the news to people he had just met, instead of Dad's gastroenterologist or primary care physician. This interaction could have been so much better for both the doctor and the patient.

My mother was confused and upset and did not know what to make of the information. When we asked for more details, the hospitalist shared a few more details. Relieved when he told us there was no indication that the cancer had spread around the bile duct, we questioned him about other areas of the body. "His lungs show a small nodule, which may be an artifact since it appeared in an older X-ray." We hung on to the tiny bit of good news and thanked the young hospitalist. But the next interaction left us with more questions than answers.

A conversation with the nurse practitioner from the gastroenterology practice, during her hospital rounds, was even more distressing than the delivery of the news by the hospitalist. She looked at my mom calmly and made a statement in a matter-of-fact tone about not really needing to bother with any form of life-saving measures or other treatment because of my father's age. My mom did not think she understood the nurse practitioner. What did she mean when she asked, "No life-saving measures or treatment, correct?" Why wouldn't we take life-saving measures? The nurse practitioner left, and we learned why, several months later, she had asked those questions.

Cholangiocarcinoma was the name of the cancer that would curse us for the next seven months. Not having any familiarity with this type of cancer, I looked up several articles on it. I studied these carefully, looking for any bright spots. Often known as cancer of the bile duct or biliary cancer, this was a type of cancer involving the main branches of the liver that touch multiple other organs in the digestive tract. I read that if the tumor was found to have a type of abnormal FGFR2 gene, my father might be a candidate for a newer form of treatment. The genomic test would look for a change in the genome that may have caused my father to develop cholangiocarcinoma. With this initial research, I grew enthusiastic about the potential possibility of a pill that could address Dad's cancer. Not surprisingly, Dad was less concerned with his diagnosis and more concerned about his family.

Immediately after being informed of the diagnosis, Dad's attention went to only his loved ones. He was deeply concerned about Mom and how she would go on if he left this world. During his first hospital stay, he turned to my older sister and asked that she take care of my mom. My father and mother were remarkably close. She was his bride—the one woman he had picked out of the ten he visited with his uncle in Iran when it was time to find the perfect woman to marry. He had a deep love for her. My mom showed her deep love for my father by taking care of him, his children, and the home. Her father died when she was young. He was known to be a stoic man. Like her father, Mom was also a stoic woman, seldom showing her feelings of love and devotion for my father by way of public displays of affection. But surprisingly, this changed rapidly during my father's illness.

My mother's reaction to the diagnosis was remarkable. I thought she would fall apart and we would need to support her more than my father. Poised and determined, she impressed me with her positive attitude and ability to smile at my father when she was crying inside. She looked at my dad and gently stroked the back of his head, and said, "Bahram, we are going to fight it." From that day on, she never left his side. She was with him in the hospital, sleeping next to him on an uncomfortable chair or on a couch near the bed if she was lucky.

My father's illness tore my world apart, and seeing my mother's silent suffering made it even more painful. Mom is not one to talk about her feelings or confide in friends about her fears. She was trying to be strong and would seldom let herself become emotional when we were around. It is extremely difficult to watch a suffering parent with a terminal illness. Watching their partner of fifty-five years suffer just as much is unbearable.

Our younger sister was unclear about the diagnosis. Like all of us, she was just trying to process the new information. Unlike my older sister and me, she did not work in health care and pharma, so she was not as quick to recognize the terms the physicians used during the process of diagnosis. As the news became grimmer, she came to realize the gravity of the situation but remained in a support role, trying to assist with any logistics that she could manage.

Ironically, though my older sister and I differed on some issues, we were similar in many ways. At the beginning of my father's illness, we were on the same page. As the first option, we planned to contact experts around the country to explore surgery to remove what appeared to be an isolated tumor. We both thought he would be fine. Neither of us was considering what may happen if surgery failed. It was too early for that, and neither of us was ready to accept defeat at this point. We were open to anyone's advice, especially my father's physician friends, who came to see him during his hospitalization. Hope was the winning attitude, and with today's progress in medicine and technology, we were certain that this would be merely a bump on the road.

Operation "Save Dad" began with everyone aligned after hearing the diagnosis while rejecting the prognosis. The entire family was rooting for him to emerge victorious from his battle with this rare cancer. We pulled out our Rolodexes and engaged with medical professionals and cancer centers familiar with this cancer, believing in the adage, "Where there is a multitude of counselors lies wisdom." Additionally, we planned to have a consult with the surgeon in the system where my father had practiced. We were cautiously optimistic about the local surgeon but considered Memorial Sloan as our first choice for any treatment or surgery.

Our initial experience in the hospital highlighted the less-than-ideal interaction during the delivery of a terminal diagnosis. This encounter represented one of many reasons why so many providers and patients alike believe the healthcare system in its current state is broken in our country. The lack of continuity, the absence of clear communication between providers, and the shortage of compassion and guidance when delivering news regarding a terminal diagnosis were all alarming to me as an individual familiar with the healthcare system. This experience was contrary to how things worked when my dad was still seeing his own patients in the hospital. These first interactions were just the beginning of a series of poor interactions layered with meeting some incredibly hard-working and passionate individuals trapped in a very flawed healthcare system.

Chapter 6

A Meaningful Existence

After my separation in 2018, I promptly moved to the city from the suburbs of Boston, where I could be closer to friends, and within walking distance of the university I had just enrolled in for my master's. Instead of contemplating the divorce after twenty-three years of marriage, I decided to focus on personal growth. I have questioned coincidences in my life multiple times and still wonder if coincidences truly exist. Dad was diagnosed in September 2019, just as I was also starting my last year of graduate studies. One of my required courses was "Hospice, Palliative Care, and End-of-Life." It was quite strange that I just happened to take this required course when it was available, coinciding with the timing of my father's diagnosis. In this class, we were learning so much about end of life, death, and dying, all concepts that were foreign to me. As a first-generation American, I was still uncomfortable with these topics even though I identified much more with the American culture. The course I was taking introduced us to multiple cultures and views on death and dying. Topics like a good death, a meaningful existence, and the end of life were topics we avoided when I was growing up. It was not surprising that these topics were still uncomfortable for me to discuss in class among my peers.

It was unimaginable that in a few months, I would be living the scenarios we had read about and discussed in class. Was this God's way of helping me through this horrific journey? Reliance on so many of the concepts helped me get through the darkest times during my father's illness. I am still so grateful to my professor, who was an angel in disguise throughout this time. All too familiar with the loss of a loved one to the same terminal illness, my professor continued to check on my mental health throughout the course of Dad's illness, advising me on real-time matters. I am not sure if she knew it, but she helped me through this dark time of my life more than she will ever know. For me, the footprint in the sand was this woman carrying me during a time when I could barely walk.

During the same palliative care course, I was most impressed with one of our guest speakers, someone I have come to admire deeply from afar. Prior to her lecture, I had not really given the topic much thought, but her story opened my eyes to what the words "meaningful existence" may mean to each of us.

Amy Berman was the invited lecturer during the fall semester to speak on "A Meaningful Existence." She is a senior program officer with The John A. Hartford Foundation, working on the development and dissemination of innovative, cost-effective models of care that improve health outcomes for older adults. Amy also leads many of the foundation's efforts focused on serious illness and end of life, including efforts to support palliative care. What is even more admirable about her is that she is a nurse and a decade-long survivor of stage IV inflammatory breast cancer. Her lecture was eye-opening, inspiring, and informative.

Since her diagnosis, she has set clear expectations for herself and others, defining what makes up a "meaningful" existence for her, and when that existence is no longer acceptable. Ms. Berman mentioned that she tells her providers she wants to have the Niagara Falls effect, meaning that she wants to continue life doing all the things that bring her joy, such as travel and work. When she gets to a point where the disease dictates her life and her quality of life is significantly diminished, she will be ready to end her life. She chose minimal therapy, one that would be the least toxic, immunotherapy with side effects she has adapted to and now is able to tolerate. Dealing with the minor side effects, Amy has found her new baseline, which includes some of the daily aches and pains that come with cancer. She has beaten all the odds relating to survival. Her positive attitude and clarity about what she desires and what she does not at the end of life, are apparent and will make it far easier for her family, significant other, and friends. Choosing to end her life when she is about to "tip over Niagara Falls" has given her more control over her destiny. Death with dignity, to Amy, is being in the presence of family and friends and controlling the end rather than being controlled by the forces of her disease. Her bravery is extraordinary, though the decisions involving death and dying are never easy.

During the course, I was constantly reminded that mortality is never an easy topic to discuss among family members and loved ones. Preparing for death does not always mean it is immediate. It only means it is eminent. We are all mortal and preparing for death is preparing for a journey to the next phase of existence. There are many ways to prepare, both psychologically and physically. Many cultures encourage end-of-life discussions in the context of terminal illness so that loved ones can inform family members of their wishes should they become incapacitated. In studying the topic, it was revealing to learn about the level of death anxiety being directly correlated with one's belief in an afterlife. Those who believe in an afterlife have the lowest level of death anxiety as opposed to people who do not believe in any form of life after life is over on this Earth. A family's reaction to the news of terminal illness is often based on culture and attitude toward end of life.

I was always impressed with the way my in-laws handled this topic. They were of German descent and vastly different than my own parents in their attitudes about death and dying. While they enjoyed life to the fullest, they accepted and prepared for death. They believed in an afterlife in heaven or hell, centered on behaviors during life on Earth. During one of our visits to their home, they presented their son with a thick folder. It included their will, proxy, and paperwork for a gravesite, along with the receipt for the fully paid funeral arrangements. This was astonishing to me. It would never be anything I would experience with my parents and our Persian culture. A mere hint at a discussion about death would be shunned as a completely inappropriate topic. As a result, when my father was diagnosed, none of these topics had been previously discussed, so we were all trying to figure out the best path forward without ever having discussed my father's wishes or how he wanted to spend his remaining days. Honestly, I think we all thought that we had more time with Dad, so discussing end-of-life plans, even after his diagnosis, was not necessary.

Tensions grew as my father's cancer progressed. We became uber-focused on the current state and the urgency of each situation, which made it impossible to have conversations about Dad's future desires. The window for an amiable and transparent discussion, where Dad expressed his wishes, suddenly closed. As was the case with our family, so many families are surprised and unprepared when their loved one suddenly becomes ill and deteriorates quickly. What we learned the hard way was that the conversations about healthcare decisions should have taken place earlier.

Not having clarity about what Dad would want during each stage of his illness made it difficult for the family to agree on the next steps. Dad was asked whom he would like to have as his designated proxy after his diagnosis, prior to his first procedure. It was not clear whether this proxy was for the procedure he was about to have or if it applied to the duration of his illness. Mom's wish was to delegate this responsibility to my older sister. Everything happened quickly, and there was no time to have the entire family provide input into this decision. Mom and Dad had been together for decades, and she knew him better than anyone else, so shouldn't Mom have been his proxy, even if she had to ask us questions about terms or information she did not understand? I was puzzled by this decision but trusted that we would look for the best path and make decisions about Dad's health as a family if he were no longer able to make these decisions.

We had been so close, after the initial surprise, I never gave this much thought. To me, it felt as though Mom should have been the proxy, even if it was just a formality. My sister was a natural leader, self-confident, and capable of asking questions and understanding medical terminology. Certainly, I believed she would act on behalf of the family. Looking back, I realize that the challenges we faced later were related to a lack of alignment on the first decision, the designation of the proxy, and what it would mean.

From early in the diagnosis, my older sister and I were determined to extend Dad's life. Initially, we both wanted him to declare war on his cancer and win. We shared an intense emotional connection to Dad, and the fact that we had never discussed his wishes beforehand did not matter. As this journey continued, we each thought we knew what he wanted based on our own assumptions.

What we had no idea about was how much treatment he was willing to receive, and under what conditions he would want to continue to try to extend his life, versus comfort measures that would focus on the quality of life, not quantity. Foolishly, I trusted that my sister and I were going to agree. When Dad was asked about his health goals at his surgeon's appointment, he indicated that he would like to be alive for one to two years to enjoy seeing more of his family, especially his grandchildren. Yet, we were not clear on what would be an acceptable and meaningful existence beyond those statements. Escalating tensions were the direct result of our failure to confirm we were on the same page regarding Dad's wishes if his disease progressed.

Unfortunately, many families face multiple crossroads during a loved one's illness, and sometimes both quality of life and extension of life cannot coexist, as we came to find out in Dad's case. Starting the discussion when he was already dealing with his illness was not feasible because of the intensity of emotions involved as we focused on immediate decisions. What if he thought we had already given up on him or did not believe there was a possibility of survival? We did not want him to give up, but that also meant that we were not always being realistic about what was possible in terms of quality of life and long-term survival.

Why is it so difficult for us to discuss the topic of death with our loved ones? Death is imminent. That we know to be true for certain. Acceptance of one's mortality may be the first step toward preparing for an unexpected illness. Planning for end-of-life based on our individual desires is simply assisting our loved ones in the decision-making process. One way to begin the conversation with loved ones is to inform them about your own preferences and your interpretation of a meaningful existence. Though it may sound peculiar, an ideal time to have a dialogue with family is during holiday gatherings where hypothetical situations can be presented. Emotions may drive decisions during desperate times when a loved one is ill, leading to more torment and anguish for patients and families alike. Detangling emotions from logic may become more difficult during a health crisis.

For our family and many others, the omission of important discussions around illness, death, and dying has meant deep division and struggles between family members on the optimal course of action. As resentment builds, families struggle to make even the simplest decisions regarding care. This was true in our case.

General agreement among family members during the decision-making process becomes exceedingly important when a loved one can no longer process the information for themselves. Even in the initial stages of Dad's illness, our family was divided, with each member pushing what they believed to be the right approach to obtaining medical opinions. Sometimes Dad would verbalize his dismay, observing the friction between us sisters, by stating, "I am only one patient surrounded by many doctors."

It is critical to maintain harmony among family members and avoid additional stress and anxiety for the patient. Mental health and wellness are critical to both the patient and family members as they embark on the battle of survival amid a terminal diagnosis, trying to find a balance between quality of life and realistic life expectancy.

Chapter 7

When the Doctor Becomes the Patient

While my dad was recovering from the infection and processing the news about his diagnosis, my sister and I had already begun our research. My mother's cousin, a famous general surgeon in California, was promptly contacted by my sister. I contacted some of my physician friends in Boston, asking them for resources and where to go for second opinions. Memorial Sloan Kettering in NYC quickly opened a patient record. The efficiency of their system is better than any other system I have ever dealt with. They had a case manager who was the single point of contact for us and a connection to both surgeons and medical oncology departments at the cancer hospital. Within a few days, Memorial Sloan Kettering retrieved all my father's blood tests, CT scans, X-rays, and physician notes through the electronic health record (EHR) system. This was an impressive use of EHR technology. Downloading pages and pages of scans and tests happened in a matter of seconds, allowing multiple experts in NYC to view them and make recommendations.

We had an appointment secured at Memorial Sloan for early October 2019. My sister and I were unstoppable, communicating on what seemed to be a telepathic level as we secured doctor appointments near and far and downloaded information about experts in the field for my father to get a third or even fourth opinion. Mom was an enthusiastic fan of our research. She liked having a lot of data prior to making any decisions. We were certainly supplying ourselves with a wealth of information about the next steps. My younger sister was collating information and organizing everything into files for future reference. Trained as a teacher, she was particularly good at this. It seemed quite therapeutic for her, especially during stressful periods.

As the first step, a temporary stent was placed to prevent the recurrence of blockage of the bile duct where the tumor was located. Endoscopic retrograde cholangiopancreatography (ERCP) is used as both lifesaving and palliative measures, combining endoscopy and X-rays to visualize the bile ducts, collect biopsy specimens, and provide either temporary or permanent treatment for pancreatic and liver diseases. It requires a gastroenterologist with experience in these procedures, as not all are trained to perform ERCP. Although the procedure is typically short, often no longer than one hour, the stent must be placed precisely to ensure stability and prevent post-procedure complications. There are several types of stents available to use. In plain language, the plastic stent is placed as a temporary measure, and the wire stents are considered a destination or permanent therapy. The plastic stent was deemed the best option for Dad since we were certain that surgical treatment to remove the cancer in the bile duct was our best path forward. We were advised about the potential complications of a plastic stent moving or causing more infections.

Still, we were not interested in hearing about that because our goal was to have Dad in surgery within a month. Dad was discharged from the hospital after a few days and seemed to be feeling okay and was in good spirits. Persian food was Dad's favorite. Mom made sure there was plenty of it around after his discharge. We were grateful to see Dad recovering well from the bile duct infection and stent placement, smiling, and enjoying his food. Returning to baseline after infections and procedures can be challenging for octogenarians. Dad's stellar attitude and determination helped him bounce back quickly. Our celebration of Dad's rapid recovery was suddenly interrupted by another infection, rearing its ugly head.

Dad's violent shaking in bed woke Mom up. When she checked on him, she knew he was not okay. Dad had a high fever, chills, and uncontrollable shivering. The shivering resembled convulsions. My younger sister was with them and immediately called 9-1-1. She covered Dad with blankets, wrapping every inch of his body. Then she quickly activated the instant heat packs, tucking them into corners to help make Dad more comfortable. The shaking continued as he was whisked away by the ambulance to the same hospital he had left just a few days prior.

Although we were warned about the potential complications of the stent placement, we never expected Dad to be back in the hospital so soon after the procedure. Nor did we expect him to be violently ill. His fever was over 102 degrees, and the shaking continued as Dad was wheeled into the emergency room, where they quickly started the antibiotics. The stent was replaced in the next day or two. This meant going under anesthesia once again to have the original stent replaced. The stent can impede the efficient movement of the bile through the bile duct. The new stent would be a bit different in size and shape, allowing the bile to pass through with a lower risk of infection. We were desperate and needed to buy time with the new stent to bridge Dad to surgery. The gastroenterologist suggested a medication to dilute the bile and prevent infection only when my brother-in-law pressed him about a medication to prevent another infection.

Time was not on our side as we investigated our travel options to NYC's Memorial Sloan Kettering. We would see two surgeons for a consult for my father. As soon as Dad was released from the hospital, we knew Memorial Sloan might be too far for him to travel. He was moving slowly and looked a little weak as he recovered from two bouts of sepsis and two procedures in ten days. We decided to see the local liver transplant surgeon and an expert in bile duct cancer. We made the appointment quickly, convinced that speeding up surgery was crucial.

During the pre-op appointment, the surgeon explained the procedure and how they would remove the portions of the bile duct where the tumor had grown. Healthy sections of the bile ducts would be reattached once the tumor was removed. The incision for this operation would be large as the approach to this type of surgery is referred to as "open" abdominal surgery rather than laparoscopic, where a few small incisions are made. I was a little surprised to hear the laparoscopic technology would not be utilized here and asked about it at the appointment. After researching the topic, I noted that the Mayo Clinic, rated as one of the best hospitals for the management of cholangiocarcinoma, had been using the laparoscopic approach for years. Although laparoscopic surgery has many advantages over the "open" surgical approach, individual surgeons have their own preferences based on their training, skill, comfort level, and the location of the tumor. In our surgeon's case, he may not have been comfortable with the laparoscopic approach or felt it was not optimal in Dad's case.

Sadly, there was no time for travel or second opinions. We needed to decide quickly. One more question from Mom stands out in my memory from that day. She asked two brilliant questions during the consultation with the local surgeon. Her questions concerned failure rates and the presence of cancer beyond the bile ducts. His response was just what we wanted to hear. There was about a one to three percent chance that he would find more cancer even if the scans had shown no other signs of cancer around the bile ducts. He was a transplant and oncological hepatobiliary surgeon with an excellent reputation. The possibility of another infection deterred us from getting a second opinion. Given the circumstances, we decided Dad would have surgery in Rochester, NY.

The morning of surgery arrived. Dad woke up that morning complaining of chills. He was not shaking as he had been previously, but he complained about similar symptoms. A low-grade fever was detected when my mom took his temperature, but fortunately, it was not high enough to cause the violent shaking. My older sister smiled and reminded Dad of his scheduled surgery that morning. We had no time for the brewing infection. The entire family accompanied Dad to the hospital.

Enthusiasm for positive news after surgery preoccupied our family's minds as we kissed Dad on his way to the operating room. Dad would soon be on the mend, or so we thought. In fact, I recall being in jovial spirits in the patient waiting area, confident that the illness was only a blip on the screen for Dad and that he would be well again in no time. Dad's diagnosis was devastating for all of us. For the first time in weeks, we had hope for a cure.

None of us were ready to let go of this aspiration or accept anything but good news. The spiritual and physical universes had different plans. We received an early call from the operating room, letting us know that surgery had begun and it was proceeding as planned, allowing us a momentary sigh of relief. The calm that followed the call was brief, interrupted by a second call from the operating room to the patient waiting area. "The surgeon would like to meet with your family immediately," exclaimed one of the waiting area receptionists. We looked up, surprised by the message. Our family was led to a private conference room at the corner of the large waiting room. Anxiously awaiting the surgeon, we realized that having been called into a conference room only a couple of hours into the operation was not a good sign.

My heart was beating so hard that I could almost hear it. My face was flushed. You could hear a pin drop as we all looked at each other, desperately praying for positive news. None of us expected or anticipated sad news, nor were we ready to accept such news. The few minutes before the surgeon entered the room seemed like hours. He looked defeated but deliberate as he pulled up a chair and sat closest to Mom. The surgeon broke the news as gently as he could, drawing a picture of the liver and bile ducts and explaining why removal of the cancerous area was impossible. He informed us that the area impacted by the tumor was much larger than anticipated and that lymph nodes around the hepatobiliary area appeared diseased. The cancer had spread to the surrounding tissues. Resection was no longer a viable path.

Our hopes and dreams of saving Dad were shattered. The collective tears running down our faces could have filled the small conference room. The tears turned to sobs that grew increasingly audible. This reaction to the news led the surgeon to continue the discussion to ensure we understood why he was making the recommendation to abort surgery. Our bearer of unwelcome news explained that removal of the bile duct and the tissues surrounding it would necessitate performing a much more lengthy and complex surgery called Whipple. In this procedure, he would need to remove the head of the pancreas, a part of the small intestine, a part of the liver, the gallbladder, and bile duct. He continued, knowing at least one person in the room needed him to go on. "Your dad has a fatty liver caused by high cholesterol levels. Typically, a liver will regrow after surgery. But in your dad's case, the liver is in barely acceptable condition." The skepticism in the room was palpable.

The air in the room grew thicker by the second. When the surgeon explained what the tissue around the bile duct looked and felt like, I had no more questions. I agreed with the recommendation to abort the surgery and wanted the surgeon to get right back into the operating room to close Dad's incision.

Unconvinced, my sister asked for more information on the Whipple. The surgeon remained calm, understanding the plea was out of desperation, and explained, "Your father may survive the Whipple surgery, but he will not make it out of the hospital alive due to his age, length of surgery, the status of the liver, and the proximity of the tumor to the pancreas. Performing the Whipple will remove significant disease, yet we have not cured your father because the cancer is already in the lymph nodes around the bile duct." The surgeon agreed to biopsy the cells around the region to ensure the results validated his findings. To his credit, he summoned two of his partners to the operating room for their opinions. Turning my attention away from the doctor, I glanced at Mom, noticing she had just aged a decade in the last ten minutes. My younger sister embraced her, trying to offer reassurance. Mom was clearly in shock, visibly shaken, and struggled to fight the tears running down her face. I am not sure she heard anything after the first few sentences. The air in the room was still.

I struggled to understand my sister's position and why she questioned a skilled surgeon's opinion. Perhaps it was not the surgeon; he was only the messenger. It was the news he delivered that we were all having a tough time processing. My younger sister asked the question that may have crossed my mind eventually. But I certainly was not ready for it when it came up. "What is his prognosis?" The response stayed with me like a bad dream. "Your father has a couple of months to live," the surgeon murmured before walking out of the room with his head down.

We left the conference room, visibly shaken and distraught, clenching stale, wet tissues in our hands. The walls of the waiting room began to close in as I walked over to sit with the rest of my family. Consoling one another was futile. Minutes ticked by on the clock on the wall, now more audible, as we waited to hear from the operating room. Two hours seemed like two days as we waited for notification of when we could see Dad. Instructions on the door warned that only two family members could enter the intensive care unit. Heartbroken and oblivious to our surroundings, we walked right through the doors and over to where Dad was lying with his eyes closed. What would we say when he opened his eyes? I dreaded the moment he would find out what had happened. We agreed not to discuss the details of the surgery with Dad. News about the failed surgery was to be kept to ourselves to allow Dad to regain his strength first. Well, at least that was the plan. What we forgot was that Dad was exceptionally astute.

Reality suddenly stung me about how surgery may not have been the best path. Dad lay still with multiple tubes, IVs, and large monitors beeping next to him. It did not take long after he opened his eyes to survey the room and notice that we had all been crying. He was grimacing with pain as he pivoted toward my older sister and said, "So, were they able to do everything they wanted? It does not look like it based on all the sad faces in this room!" His eyes welled up as he tried to be strong and stoic. Soon, we were all crying about the unspoken words floating in the sterile, dark room.

I felt nauseous. My legs felt lifeless and weak. Ashamed that we could not contain our feelings, I lowered my head and began to stare at the floor to avoid eye contact. Without saying a word, we informed him of the dismal course ahead. Earlier that morning, I had envisioned the celebration of his successful surgery. Now I felt powerless, standing there unable to help my father, the man I had loved and admired all my life. But he astonished us once again, knowing just what to say. Dad reassured us it would be up to the guy above as he looked up at the ceiling.

The following weeks were about Dad's recovery and decisions about the next steps. Most importantly, the plastic stent would need to be replaced with a permanent metal stent as soon as Dad had enough strength to undergo another procedure under anesthesia. A medical oncology consult seemed reasonable to explore options to extend Dad's life. We underestimated the length of recovery from big open surgery in an eighty-five-year-old with multiple comorbidities. Dad had survived two bouts of sepsis prior to his surgery. Each hospitalization made it more difficult to return to his baseline. Stacking the surgery on top of the previous hospitalizations took its toll on Dad's body.

Pain, infection, and bleeding are three most common complications after abdominal surgery. Fortunately, the hospital used the regional anesthesia team for Dad's surgery. Nerve blocks have been used for many years to reduce pain in the surgical site and surrounding area. I remember rotating with an anesthesiologist during my graduate studies in pain management. He would exclaim, "If there is a nerve to block, I will block it," referring to using nerve blocks prior to surgery. Nerve blocks can effectively reduce postoperative pain by preventing the nerve from signaling the pain receptors. A transversus abdominis plane (TAP) block was used in Dad's case to block the nerves that provide sensation and muscle function of the abdominal wall and skin. This block provided significant pain relief immediately after his surgery. The downside to these blocks is they often wear off quickly, and the patient response is variable based on anatomy, the extent of the surgical area, and the skill of the provider. The addition of a non-opioid IV medication enabled Dad to begin to walk back and forth to the bathroom with the help of a walker. I was an enthusiastic fan of using non-narcotic medication. Delirium, sedation, and urinary retention are just a few of many possible adverse events with narcotics. Sadly, the hospital protocol limited the use of IV non-narcotic medication to two days.

Per protocol to be followed for all abdominal surgeries, the resident and the attendings rounding on my father discontinued his IV pain medication. Disappointed by this decision, we were determined to advocate for Dad and push for the medication that had been effective and well-tolerated. The blessing of a third day of the IV non-narcotic was due to the efforts of a young cardiac surgery fellow rotating with the transplant surgeon. When we told him about our wish to continue the medication, he was able to get authorization for an additional day. Cardiac surgeons typically have more flexibility to override protocols and individualize treatments. The young surgeon was Persian and mentioned that Dad reminded him of his grandfather. What he did for us was what he would have done for his grandfather. He rounded on

Dad every day after his surgery. But he would return after his shift just to check in with Dad and spend time with him. Dad was easy to admire. This young doctor quickly became fond of Dad.

By the fourth day after surgery, Dad was started on an oral narcotic and oral acetaminophen. With the first dose of the oral narcotic, Dad's eyes got heavy after breakfast. He took an exceptionally long nap and had no interest in walking. In fact, he slept most of that day, barely getting up to eat or drink anything. He grimaced each time we helped him sit up and was obviously in significant pain. Dad had done so well without any narcotics. He moved around, was alert, and ate well. The family had a routine of "walking with Papa" several times a day, where one or two grandchildren would line up behind Dad, pushing a chair behind him in case he had to rest and cheering him on to keep walking the halls. This activity was no longer appealing to Dad.

Shortly after the initiation of the oxycodone, Dad stopped urinating as regularly as he had been. He developed urinary retention on the second morning after starting the narcotic. The bladder scan showed a large amount of urine in the bladder. To deal with the urinary retention, the staff had to drain the urine with a catheter to make Dad more comfortable and prevent infection.

This is not a pleasant procedure. And the discomfort was exacerbated by the incisional pain, which continued to limit Dad's mobility. Though sleepy and less alert, he was still feeling intense pain, which continued to be poorly controlled by the narcotics. We tried to be present when the doctors rounded each day. My older sister and I reported Dad's response to the new medication during rounds and inquired whether the IV non-narcotic could be reordered. The doctors mentioned that the hospital pharmacy had an issue with the "overuse" of the drug and that the hospital's CPOE (computerized patient order entry) system would not allow them to reorder the drug.

While the doctors agreed that the urinary retention may have been a direct result of the narcotic use, their preference was to try another oral medication, which they called a "gentler" narcotic, called Tramadol. Dad continued to have significant pain, but later that evening, he began to deteriorate, exhibiting new symptoms.

Just prior to dinner, I noticed Dad was getting more uncoordinated. When I helped him to walk to the bathroom, his legs were hyperextended, and his muscles were stiff. His heart rate and blood pressure were up and increasing at a steady pace. Most alarming was his change of affect and disposition. Suddenly, he became very agitated and frustrated with the inability to move his legs effectively. He sank back into the bed after a few attempts. I had to help him use the plastic urinal to empty his bladder. When he laid back in bed, I noticed he was sweating through his hospital gown. Dad's eyes widened, and he looked around, confused and disoriented. I grew extremely concerned, wondering what was causing these changes.

I was alone with Dad during this incident. My older sister had just left for dinner with her family, and my mom and younger sister were at the hospital cafeteria, grabbing us a quick bite to eat. It even occurred to me that I may be imagining Dad's symptoms, but they continued, and I knew I needed to get help. After ringing the nurse button to call a provider, I began to google Dad's new medications and look for any potential drug-drug interactions. Serotonin syndrome was listed on product inserts of the two drugs that Dad was taking. Each product label recommended avoidance of concomitant use with the other drug due to the considerable risk of interaction and the risk of serotonin syndrome. The Tramadol product label had warnings about multiple drug interactions. I immediately surmised that the addition of this drug was the possible cause of Dad's new symptoms.

Tramadol was immediately discontinued, and oxycodone was started once again. Dad experienced increased pain after the Tramadol was discontinued. The process of changing medications is not simple. New orders must be approved, and the assigned nurse needs to interrupt what they are doing to administer the new medication. Dad's pain escalated in the meantime, causing him severe discomfort. The oxycodone was finally started again, with negligible impact on his pain. Within fifteen minutes, Dad was dozing off, only to wake a few minutes later, complaining of pain. A pain consult was requested for the next day to try to resolve the ongoing discomfort. Again, my sister and I enthusiastically asked for the IV acetaminophen and told the team how well Dad was doing on that regimen. They did not respond except to say, "Tramadol can be a dirty drug." Sadly, it did not seem like there was a path to managing Dad's pain effectively. I knew if we could only get him to move about more, he would feel better. But the drowsiness was a limiting factor.

Fever set in the next morning. Dad should have been doing much better several days into his recovery. Instead, he was exhausted, with little, if any, appetite. When the blood tests from the night before came back, they showed a brewing infection. After further tests, it was determined that the bacteria were present in the urinary tract and bladder. Was this a direct result of urinary retention or the use of the catheter to drain the urine? Or was it just a pure coincidence? We had our own opinions, but there was no time to contemplate. By the next day, additional bacteria were detected in his blood. This bacterium was identified as the type that typically grows in the abdomen. Both gram-negative and gram-positive bacteria were culprits in slowing Dad's recovery. Unfortunately, sensitivities and allergies to several antibiotics narrowed options for treating the infections.

A PICC line, a peripherally inserted central venous catheter, was inserted to ensure an IV route was available post-discharge. It served as the mechanism for administering this drug for the next several weeks. My younger sister was the lucky trainee who would learn to give the drug once Dad was discharged. Since she had temporarily moved into my parent's home, it made sense for her to take this on. She quickly trained as a caregiver and administered the drug for the entire duration of treatment after Dad's discharge. Everyone appreciated her courage to take this on.

Coexisting infections derailed our plans for Dad's rapid discharge from the hospital. We settled for having the infection addressed and treated quickly. Dad's pain continued to limit his mobility, and he became less interested in his daily walks around the hallways. From that point on, he was completely reliant on his walker. Visually, this was a new norm, a new baseline for Dad. He was a healer for fifty-five years of his life. We were not used to seeing him lean into a walker. Seeing him become weaker was heartbreaking. It was unnatural for him to be the patient. Fortunately, he had mastered adversity in the past and was adaptable, and seemed to handle his new norm better than all of us.

Dad maintained his clever sense of humor, no matter how he felt. Always smiling when anyone from his care team entered the room, he would take the time to ask how their day was going. He would always thank them for coming to see him. From the cleaning staff to the rounding doctors, he would greet everyone and thank them for what they were doing. One of the nurses who learned Dad was a cardiologist asked him about her irregular heartbeat. She told Dad she had her EKG, a tracing of the heart rhythm. Ecstatic that Dad had offered to read it and explain it to her, she brought her tracing in for him to review with her. I watched him carefully go through the EKG with this young nurse and show her what to look for and how to recognize abnormalities on the strip and what each segment signified. Watching Dad interact with people was a lesson every day, a lesson in kindness, compassion, and thoughtfulness. Regardless of how badly he felt, he was grateful to be with his family and cared for by his providers.

While he enjoyed having us around immensely during his hospitalization, he often had to remind us it was time for him to retire for the night. We all had a habit of piling into the tiny room, borrowing chairs from the staff, and settling in for hours, waiting for any task that needed to be performed to assist Dad. When all our families were in town, Dad's room tended to get quite crowded. We knew it was time to go when Dad turned to us with his unforgettable smile and said, "Thank you for coming."

I rarely heard him complain. On good days, when Dad had an appetite, he even enjoyed eating the mediocre food served at the hospital. Mom spent day and night at the hospital, taking only a short break to go home to shower, change, and make Dad some homemade soup or bring his favorite snacks. She brought his favorite hot cocoa for his morning caffeine and anything else she thought he would enjoy eating. Dad was lactose intolerant. As a treat, Mom would bring him his special dairy-free yogurt with some fresh fruit. Sometimes she would surprise him with his favorite dairy-free ice cream, though he was not to eat too much of it because of his type 2 diabetes. Hiding behind her smile and forced laughter in his presence were her fear and anxiety, both eating away at her as the pounds dropped off her body and wrinkles became more pronounced. As I watched the aging process in fast forward, it was obvious that she was internalizing the pain that came with the thought of losing my father.

After the failed surgery, there was yet another procedure to be performed prior to his discharge. Replacement of the plastic stent with a metal stent was recommended despite the ongoing infection. Since antibiotics were already on board, the preference was to have this procedure scheduled as soon as possible and before the plastic stent caused another infection. To prepare for another ERCP, eating or drinking at least twelve hours before the procedure was prohibited. The team was quite strict about the rule, not allowing anything to be ingested except a small sip for oral meds starting at midnight prior to the day of the procedure.

Dad's type two diabetes was very well controlled prior to his illness. Starting with the very first procedure and later for his surgery, steroids were utilized as prophylaxis for post-procedure or postoperative nausea and vomiting. The negative impact of steroids on blood glucose levels in patients with a history of type two diabetes, when utilized perioperatively, is controversial. Only the endocrinology providers rounding on Dad seemed to think his blood glucose levels were off due to the multiple doses of steroids he had received in a span of a few weeks. As expected, during Dad's recovery from surgery, his glucose levels were up and down like a seesaw. When the glucose levels dropped too low because of too much insulin or too little food, he began to break out in a cold sweat and feel faint and nauseous. He needed to eat immediately to feel better. Fasting prior to procedures was especially tough on Dad because of how low glucose impacted him physically.

The gastroenterology fellow came by the morning of the procedure and informed the family that the case would be scheduled for some time that afternoon. The gastroenterology lab was set up to take care of outpatients with appointments and fit in the inpatients when they had gaps in the schedule. There were no openings earlier, regardless of our insistence to have Dad scheduled as soon as possible due to the issues with his glucose levels when fasting.

This meant that Dad was on standby for an opening in the schedule for his procedure. Imagine for a moment that you are terminally ill, recovering from major surgery, fighting significant infections with unstable glucose levels, and now you are told you are not to eat or drink until you are notified, adding hunger pains to the alphabet soup of ailments. By late afternoon, our frustration with the wait and lack of communication drove us to chase down the gastroenterology service staff members to have them commit to a time or simply delay the procedure to the next morning and allow Dad to have some food. Something was terribly wrong with how inpatients had to wait all day for a spot to open in the gastroenterology lab. We failed to reach the doctors in the gastroenterology lab, so at 6 p.m., we decided it was time to feed Dad since he had been refraining from food or water for eighteen hours. My sisters and I headed downtown and got the finest Persian kabab with rice we could find in Rochester. Watching our father enjoy a few bites was a fleeting glimpse of joy. At midnight that evening, another day of fasting began. But this time, our persistence paid off, and we managed to get the gastroenterology team to commit to a time early the next morning.

Thankfully, the procedure was completed without complications. And, of course, more steroids were administered before this procedure. Steroids are a double-edged sword in medicine. They are often utilized in perioperative settings and many other inflammatory conditions. They reduce inflammation and calm the immune system by reducing its activity. When activated by various mediators, the white blood cells help the body fight off viruses and infections. So, the timing and use of steroids must be carefully considered since they can impact the immune system's ability to fight infection. Steroids also have a profound effect on glucose control, making it even more important to weigh the risks and benefits of their use in immune-compromised patients like my father. High glucose levels are a rich breeding ground for infections. Bacteria and cancer cells thrive in a high glucose state, making elevated levels dangerous for cancer patients.

So, I understand the CMS (Centers for Medicare and Medicaid Services) guidance and mandated reporting on how well glucose levels are controlled in hospitalized diabetic patients. Yet, surprisingly, extraordinarily little attention is paid to this unless you are the endocrinology consult team managing glucose levels and responsible for reporting on this metric. To control these levels, the hospital relies solely on the short-acting insulin injected each time the glucose levels rise above a certain number.

Painstakingly, for both the patient and the nurse, glucose levels for type one and type two diabetics are measured every few hours, sometimes every hour in critically ill patients. For Dad, the levels were measured before meals and bedtime, and a sliding scale for glucose levels above a certain number informed the amount of insulin to be injected. For Dad, this meant getting stuck twice each time, once for the measurement and once for the insulin. Watching this process day after day was difficult. Each time the nurse walked in for a glucose level check, Dad winced with discomfort as they stuck yet another finger. He had needle marks and bruises everywhere. I am not convinced that any of it resulted in an improved outcome for Dad, although it may have improved scores for the hospital's glucose management metric.

Clearly, the guidelines to monitor glucose levels are well intended. However, when these guidelines are implemented, little attention is given to the patient experience or comfort level. Long-acting drugs, which he was accustomed to taking at home, may have been more appropriate and better at controlling his blood glucose. Innovative digital technology that attaches a tiny patch with a single needle prick to the patient and monitors levels around the clock would be wonderful technology. I imagine nurses would be happier not having to perform glucose checks and administering what are sometimes minute amounts of insulin.

But newer technology is not adopted quickly in hospitals. This may be just one source of frustration for providers and patients alike. These were some of the daily frustrations we all experienced at the hospital. Yet, there was not one individual to blame. These mammoth hospital systems have an incredible infrastructure, and making the smallest change requires more time and energy than any one provider or even several providers can expend.

Exhausted by surgery and the complications that ensued, Dad was finally about to be discharged on or around post-operative day nine or ten when he began to experience chills. He was trying to get dressed, with the aid of my younger sister and a nurse, when the chills took his body over, and he started shaking so badly that the bed in the room began to shake with him. Other nurses on the floor ran into the room and quickly got a hold of the infectious disease team. And, of course, it was time for more needles and more bloodwork.

The new infection lengthened his stay by another four or five days. It seemed like each time Dad began to improve, he was knocked down by another infection. We learned to focus on the positive and were grateful that we had not left the hospital when his symptoms began. After 17 long days, Dad was discharged. His recovery time was over three times the amount of time that it typically takes for a patient to be discharged from the hospital for this type of surgery. This, too, is a metric measured by the American College of Surgeons National Surgical Quality Improvement Program (NSQIP).

Trying to avoid another trip to the hospital after discharge, we managed to get the medical oncology team to see Dad for a consult regarding potential medical treatment approaches while he was still an inpatient. Prior to beginning any therapy, the team suggested testing the tumor pathology through Foundation One. For advanced cancer patients with solid tumors, this innovative company analyzes the tumor, looking for genomic signs and gene mutations to identify patients who may be a match and benefit from the FDA-approved targeted therapies. We welcomed this suggestion enthusiastically.

Hope was dimly flirtatious. The results would be back in time for our follow-up appointment with the medical oncologist to determine the best path forward for treatment. Although my older sister and I had some disagreements during Dad's first hospitalization, we generally agreed on this approach to explore further treatments. We were excited and nervous about the potential targeted therapy for Dad. I was hoping and praying for a tumor genotype match and treatment with targeted therapy, an effective and more tolerable treatment than chemotherapy for his type of cancer.

When we went to see the oncologists, Dad was still recovering from the surgery and multiple infections. He was not performing many of his daily activities, such as dressing himself, toileting, or showering. Thankfully, he was feeding himself. And with the help of a walker and a family member walking by his side, he could get himself to the kitchen and back to the bedroom, where he spent many hours sleeping. When he was in his chair in the living room, he was also often napping. The extreme fatigue was consistent with everything his body had endured in the past few weeks.

Unfortunately, there was a slight change in Dad's mental acuity. He was processing slower, like an aging computer running out of memory space. His eyes focused on the person speaking and clearly paying attention, but he would still have to think about the question and respond slowly. Most of the time, his answers made sense. Control of his glucose presented more challenges after surgery, forcing him to increase his medications. Frequent urination, another sign of his failing glucose control, was another source of discomfort. These changes were expected with the number of invasive interventions coupled with the rapidly growing cancer. It would impact most elderly patients in the same way. It was hard to imagine his deteriorating physical and mental state, let alone witness it in real-time.

Regrettably, the appointment with the medical oncology team started with the discovery that Dad's tumor was not a match for any of the more novel treatments. The feud with my older sister began shortly after this visit, fueled by her denial of the news and my grief about the future. After our visit with the medical oncologists, my hopes for treating Dad's cancer came to a crashing halt.

During that visit, it was clear that the fellow who met with the family first was hesitant to include Dad in any ongoing studies, fearing the treatments would be too harsh for him. He mentioned comfort care as the most viable option after we answered a few questions asked to gauge Dad's frailty score. One of the questions asked by the fellow had to do with the number of hours Dad was awake and alert versus asleep or inactive. I was honest when this question was asked. My older sister was disappointed with my response and disagreed. She was enthusiastic about starting the most aggressive treatment as soon as possible. Meanwhile, I questioned his physical ability to handle even the smallest dose of chemotherapy.

By the end of that appointment, it was clear that Dad was being encouraged by the family to try chemotherapy. He seemed ambivalent about it but willing to go along. The senior faculty member of the department recommended starting with a small dose of one chemotherapy agent every two weeks instead of their standard two-drug combination. The oncology team would see him after each treatment and determine how he was doing. This would continue indefinitely, with scans performed every three months to monitor his cancer. Before leaving the appointment, we mentioned that Dad had another consult at Memorial Sloan. The recommendation was to avoid the trip due to Dad's reduced functional reserve. This term refers to one's capacity to bounce back after an energy-consuming activity. In this case, it was implied that the energy spent on any long activity, such as a trip to and from New York City, would have to be weighed against its benefits. Since the doctors seemed to know each other well, we agreed with the suggestion of having Dad's oncology team in Rochester communicate directly with the Memorial Sloan physicians.

I returned to Boston for a few days after that appointment. Multiple conversations with many experts, including geriatric oncologists in Boston, made me realize that what was initially suggested regarding comfort care at the medical oncology appointment was the right path. Many of the doctors I spoke to were either friends or referred to me by friends. They sent me articles and guidelines, which I printed out to share with my family. I plowed through pages and pages of notes and literature about cholangiocarcinoma for many nights as I struggled to sleep. I would either print out or email my sister the literature, hoping that it would help her better understand what we were dealing with and why it was more important to provide Dad with treatments to help him remain as comfortable as possible. My efforts were met with resistance and rejection. My sister simply did not and would not read anything that would take away her hope for his survival and recovery from cancer. I was terrified that starting chemo would only weaken Dad more and hasten the inevitable.

Chemotherapy was the only path forward, according to my sister. She was not thrilled that the suggestion was to start with a very weak dose of a single chemo agent instead of two agents. A combination of two chemotherapy agents at doses that were studied in various bile duct cancers was her preferred approach. Generally, the studies showed a marginal improvement in survival, even with the higher doses, and did not speak to the quality of life. Like many other cancer therapy studies, the study in cholangiocarcinoma excluded octogenarians. To blast cancer hard meant having to endure side effects that may have caused a great deal of discomfort, depleting any remaining functional reserve. Higher doses of chemo might have been reasonable if Dad was younger and less frail.

Back in Rochester and visiting Dad at breakfast, a call from the medical oncologists suddenly interrupted the morning routine. I was the unlucky one to answer a phone call from Dad's physician. It was the oncology fellow, and he wanted to talk about Dad. When I tried to hand the phone to Mom, she asked me to continue speaking with the physician. I was not surprised but saddened to hear the information. After speaking with the doctor, I called my sister, who was on her way back to Rochester.

"Hi. I just wanted to let you know of some information shared by Dad's Rochester doctors this morning." I started with a calm voice. "What did they say?" she reluctantly asked. I began to speak in a guarded voice, "They have been in touch with the doctors at Memorial Sloan and went over Dad's case. The recommendation is to stay with comfort care." I could tell by the silence after my statement that my sister neither appreciated my call nor the news I had just delivered. She responded firmly with, "The chemo appointment will not be canceled. It is on for next week." I said nothing and just hung up, sorry that I had called instead of having the conversation with her in person when she arrived. Admittedly, calling my sister with unwelcome news was a terrible mistake on my part.

I always felt an obligation to share information with my sister as I received it when she was not in town. Afraid to share the news with both Mom and Dad, I chose to share the information with my mom when we were alone a little later. From that moment, my mom was pulled into the middle of the disputes with my sister. Mom's strongest desire was to protect Dad, and a close second to that was to maintain peace among the family. My sister continued to dispel Mom's doubts and looked forward to having Dad try chemo. Chemo was hope in a vial, and she was committed to trying anything to see Dad live longer. Looking back, I cannot blame her for being optimistic.

On one of the drives home from the hospital, I told my sister how I now understand why so many providers were asking Dad whether he would seek treatment for his cancer when he was diagnosed. At the time they asked, I was thinking, "How dare they assume things just because Dad is 85?" My sister looked at me, visibly frustrated, and said, "What else would we have done, just let him be and welcome death?"

I knew each word I uttered would strain our relationship more. Trying to explain my first statement, I jumped in with the question, "Would we have provided him with a better quality of life in the last month if we had opted for a permanent metal stent, dismissing the idea of a potentially curative surgery?" My statement surprised her because she felt my father's life should be extended at almost any cost. I did not say another word. Silence took over the car for the rest of the ride home.

When we decided surgery was the obvious option, we did not realize that there could be disease beyond the biliary tract in the nodes since the initial scans did not reveal the spread of the disease. In fact, we were reassured further by the surgeon during our consult that there would only be a minimal chance that he would see more extensive disease. But this type of carcinoma is extremely aggressive, and scans do not always show the extent of the disease. By the time cholangiocarcinoma is diagnosed in most cases, it has already spread to other nodes or distant organs.

Yet, the idea of giving in to cancer was not anything my sister wanted to hear or discuss. Our conversations often began calmly, escalating to harsh exchanges, followed by periods of intentional silence and avoidance of one another. My younger sister was forced to facilitate discussions between us, sometimes turning into the commander, trying to split us up by assigning us times we could be with Dad or visit him if he was in the hospital. My mother, on the other hand, impressed all of us with extraordinary strength.

Mom, still doubting her own ability to break down medical information, stayed with the decisions my sister was making. From the time my sister was designated as a proxy, she took charge of decisions made for Dad according to her own judgment. My preference would have been to reach an understanding between family members and my father so that we would all have an equal say in the way Dad's care would be managed, with my mother having the final say at each decision point.

Mom and Dad were married for decades and were inseparable. Never doubting my mother's commitment to Dad, I was now witnessing it every second of every minute of every day of his illness. It was beyond admirable. Her undying love for him grew even stronger during his illness and gave her the strength she would need to get through the next few months.

Chemo started with my sister's conviction over everyone else's ambivalence about it being the best path forward. Not present for Dad's first chemotherapy, I volunteered to take him for the baseline CT scan a few days after his treatment. Four days after the chemo, it was still difficult for my younger sister and Mom to dress him for his CT scan. He had spent the entire four days in bed, so taking him for the CT scan was a distressing experience. My sister and I had to lift his legs into the car and ease him in. It was as though the neurons were not connecting, and the signal from the brain to his limbs had become scrambled, making it difficult for him to move. Yet, after he visited the medical oncologists one week after his first chemo, my sister hailed a victory by announcing how much Dad had improved already. "Wow, the power of placebo," was the thought swirling in my head. Luckily, the thought did not transform into words. My sister was clearly convinced when she told Dad he looked better already. His mouth widened with a big smile. Hope was glistening in his eyes.

The chemo would continue next week. Steroids were prescribed to minimize the weakness after the chemotherapy, with added caution from the doctors that using steroids would expose Dad to the risk of infection and increase blood glucose levels. Dad seemed to do better with the second chemo but developed a small skin infection that was managed with topicals. Feeling braver about giving Dad steroids, my sister decided to continue them for several days after the third chemo. Dad had a heightened sensitivity to all medications. His glucose levels reached around the 400 mark and seemed uncontrollable. He was beginning to have an appreciable thirst and suffered from rashes on his tongue. His appetite for food was fading fast, along with his initial enthusiasm for chemotherapy. He remained inactive during the day. I remember the family begging him to stay up for his favorite segment of the news. He refused and bid us goodnight by exclaiming his famous phrase, "Thank you for coming." I was skeptical about the impression that chemotherapy was going well.

I cried quietly upstairs at Mom and Dad's home, wondering why we were continuing to poison him. But there was no stopping the freight train that had left the building. Nothing I could do or say would change the plans. Mom, who needed all our support, was playing referee instead and consoling me while she was equivocal herself about the decisions being made. Mere suggestions made by me were met with guerilla-strength resistance, and I was immediately accused of having ulterior motives. Why on Earth would I want to harm my father if chemo was truly helping him? Slowly, my father's once brilliant mind started to fade. Was this because of the steroids? The chemo? Cancer? Or was it a multifactorial deterioration? I will never know the answer to this question. What happened next put my relationship with my sister on permanent life support.

After spending a few days in Boston, I arrived in Rochester to visit Dad just a week after his third chemo session, and Mom decided she would run out for a quick errand. She typically never left the house if Dad was at home. She would have one of us run errands. Just after she left, my father woke up extremely confused. I quickly called my younger sister to come to Dad's room and help me assess Dad's mental status.

We asked him his name. He answered the question quickly. When we asked about his home address, he did not know and tried to guess. When we asked his age, he insisted he was one hundred twenty-five years old. We knew it was time to call our nurse at the cancer center, who recommended we take

Dad to the hospital emergency department. When Mom returned, she was equally surprised about Dad's mental status and the rapid deterioration. We spoke to my older sister by phone, who agreed with the nurse and encouraged us to take Dad to the hospital. We were unsure if he had a stroke or if the cancer had metastasized to the brain. Neither were pleasant thoughts. We called 911, and the EMT team arrived quickly, all too familiar with the address. Strong Memorial was the destination this time.

What Dad likely suffered from was chemo-induced delirium. At least this was proposed by the geriatric oncologist who rounded on him the next day. It may have been possible that cancer and the steroids had some part in it, yet his doctors were more convinced that the chemo may have had a deleterious effect on Dad. They recommended discontinuation of the chemo.

Cancer can kill, but so can chemo. While it offers hope to so many patients and has been proven to extend and even preserve the lives of many individuals, that is not the case for everyone. If used inappropriately, it can shorten the life of the patient. More importantly, chemo can negatively impact quality of life during the few short months left to live.

In my mind, the discontinuation of chemo for Dad was an example of the spiritual universe and the physical universe settling differences. Said another way, if our plan is inconsistent with the spiritual universe or what it is meant to be, the physical universe intercedes, altering the path and redirecting it to where the path was meant to be going. Mom and I could not stop the chemo. That much was clear. I had gone along with the chemo unenthusiastically, even though I felt it would harm Dad more than it would help him. Yet, his body ended up rejecting it on its own. In my mind, that was the spiritual resolution. Not according to my sister. I was responsible for the discontinuation of a life-saving therapy as she viewed it. Once again, I was the villain in the story and deserved to be treated as one.

During his fourth hospitalization for mental status change, Dad experienced delirium most of the time, thinking we were in our Florida condominium and insisting there was plenty of room for all to stay overnight. He continued to believe he was one hundred twenty-five years old and had no idea he was in a hospital. Surprisingly, on a day when we were all gathered in his room, he had a few minutes of lucidity. What he said that day continues to play in my head like an old song.

Dad could sense the ongoing friction between us and began surveying our faces as he spoke. He asked us to "make peace with one another." He looked at me with concern and said, "I am sorry for what happened to you." I knew what he meant. I said nothing and smiled. Looking at my older sister, he softly whispered, "Take care of your mother." And looking at my younger sister, he said, "He will be fine." It was clear he was only worried about his wife, children, and grandchildren. Once again, I felt shame that as the middle child and typically the peacekeeper, I had failed to maintain harmony amongst us sisters. We all began to cry.

Despite Dad's example of finding peace, my sister and I were doing anything but being peaceful. We were both trying to push our idea of the best way forward without either of us knowing exactly what my father wanted. We had never discussed death and dying as a family, even when my father first became ill. I knew my dad cherished life. But he cared for his family even more. I witnessed the level of medical intervention Dad had endured, and I knew it was not what he would have wanted. It was what he thought he should do to please his family.

Dad was discharged from the hospital after nearly two weeks. At home, we could see that he was deteriorating quickly, retaining fluid in his abdomen and walking far less. We were holding on to any positive sign. Dad's robust appetite made us hopeful. He was able to eat multiple small meals a day and enjoy his family over the next two and half months. He even joined us for both Thanksgiving dinner and Christmas celebrations. Life was like a seesaw, making us happy when Dad's mental status improved one day and sad when Dad had a bad day, appearing confused and disoriented. When asked about his age, he would go back and forth between his real age of eighty-five and one hundred twenty-five, depending on the day.

While I was grateful for every day we had with my father, my older sister was still looking for ways to intervene with invasive procedures, hoping to improve Dad's mental status and his deteriorating ability to walk, even with a walker. A new mission to heal Dad's brain was underway after the chemo was stopped. Multiple interventions took place when I was away. I had given up hope of having any suggestions accepted. Even physicians who intervened were immediately dismissed by my sister.

She made multiple appointments with neurology, urology, and others in hopes of finding some magic bullet for Dad's illness. I watched her as she talked convincingly to Dad about the next treatment or procedure. I did not realize that in my sister's mind, terminal illness did not exist for Dad. What I saw was a sister who wanted to do everything to change destiny.

My sister had not gone through the process of grieving like me. She was still in the first stage, denial, while I was in the acceptance phase and dealing with the present. I loved my sister and regretted our distasteful exchanges and accusations of each other. It was heartbreaking to read the text messages that often started with discussions about Dad's health. Our messages were venomous, vindictive, and unproductive. Indeed, I felt like I was a perfect scapegoat for channeling frustrations and anger about Dad's illness. Finally, exhausted and out of ideas to try to improve things between us, I reached out to one of my professors, asking her for advice about how to deal with the situation. She asked me to have compassion for my sister.

Looking back, I wish I had been more empathetic and showed more compassion toward her. My sister's pain was the furthest from my mind during that period. The relationship with my younger sister was also equally strained, though to a lesser degree, as she tried to manage Dad's day-to-day care, sometimes completely taking over.

It began to feel as if my older sister had completely taken over managing Dad's health, while my younger sister completely took over managing his physical care. I was left trying to manage Dad's mental well-being. His laughter and smile lit up my dark world, so I would begin joking around and singing to him as I made his green shakes every morning, just to see him smile and imitate me for a few seconds. That was enough to give me the strength to withstand unpleasant exchanges that day.

Mom was struggling with all the friction. I would find her quietly crying in her dressing area when Dad was asleep in the bedroom. She was dealing with Dad's illness and the dreadful feud between her daughters. It was an excruciatingly painful time for Mom, but she kept up pretenses, always smiling around Dad. Each time I tried to mend things or step back from getting involved in medical decisions, I was catapulted back into the battlefield in the family room, trying to stop the next intervention meant to cure the incurable.

When I was back in Boston for a few days, I continued to search and read new articles on the topic of cholangiocarcinoma, looking for anything new to give me hope. I was also desperate, seeking a miracle wonder drug to come along to help with Dad's deteriorating condition. Admittedly, I knew my efforts in this regard would be futile. Yet, I could not help immersing myself in medical literature, longing for something to come along as a viable option. Or perhaps reading was simply becoming therapeutic. What I encountered when I got home solidified my understanding of cholangiocarcinoma.

There are no coincidences in life. On a cold January morning, I headed back to Boston from Rochester to attend a weekend session for the new semester. As I checked the mail, a new copy of Surgery News lay on top of the pile of mail as if to say, "Read this now." When I picked up the January 2020 issue, I found myself instantly on page 20, reading the article with an ordinary title, "The Hardest Working Surgeon I Ever Met." When I began reading about Hiroji Noguchi, MD, a U.S.-trained transplant surgeon from Japan, I immediately saw parallels to my father's story.

This man was brilliant and hard-working, used his sense of humor to lift everyone's spirits, and did not know how to say "no" when it came to patient care. During the peak of his career in Hawaii, when life's dreams had come true, a nightmare erupted, disturbing the beauty and peace of life as he knew it. Jaundice alerted him and his colleagues that emergent diagnostic tests were in short order. He was only in his late fifties. Peers thought the jaundice was the result of a kidney or gallbladder stone. When scans revealed a hilar lesion, pointing to a more serious diagnosis of cholangiocarcinoma, his colleagues were in tears. They knew his options were limited. What played in this doctor's favor at the time was his relatively young and his otherwise excellent health.

He was able to survive the evils of radiation and chemo. These treatments bought him some time as he patiently waited on the liver transplant list. He had a successful liver transplant, but recovery was not easy for him as he struggled with transplant rejection and complications for a year. Approximately two years after his transplant, he was diagnosed with a recurrence of the same deadly cancer that had spread, with a level of metastasis that left him with only one option. He chose hospice at his home, where he died just a week later. When I finished the article, I noticed the tear stains on the paper and the rest of the mail. How could this happen to the most wonderful human being who had spent his life saving other people's lives, giving them a new liver and a second chance in life? How could God let this man's wife and children suffer a second time through this illness, followed by his death?

I sobbed as though I knew this man like I knew my father. It hit a cord with me like no other story I had ever read. Yet, I wondered if this was what God wanted me to read. Was this confirmation that putting my father through three chemo sessions and other procedures at his age, with the multiple co-morbidities, was not the right thing to do? Did we rob him of his quality of life by wanting to increase his quantity of life? These questions kept spinning around in my head all night. I finally cried myself to sleep, giving up on whether I would ever know the answer. There was no coincidence in my reading this article about Dr. Noguchi. It was meant for me to read, and I had no doubt that God was providing me his guidance through other means as he always does.

There were so many "if onlys" that I could list about my dad's final months: if only the cancer was able to be removed surgically; if only the surgical incision was not so large, causing the recovery to be so long; if only my father had not had those infections in the postoperative recovery phase; if only he were younger, then the chemo may have helped him. If only hospitals had not become for-profit businesses and physicians had more autonomy.

Peace comes with accepting the present and letting go of the past. Suffering ends when we let go of what was and accept the new norm. The word equanimity has become a permanent word tattooed in my brain. The experience of my father's terminal illness was a harsh lesson in facing the present and maintaining composure in times of chaos.

Chapter 8

Medicine Then, Medicine Now

I t was difficult to see doctors rounding on Dad without any consistency or continuity with their visits. Different partners within specialty groups were assigned to hospital rounds on different days and would see him without any kind of relationship with him. The spirit had disappeared from the building, and employees like physicians simply walked around like robots, following computer screens. Hospitals were so different than what I knew them to be like.

What I have observed over the decades in health care is an alarming transformation of medicine. The changes became more evident as I spent seven months studying this transformation. The way medicine is practiced today is unrecognizable compared to only two decades ago. The independent physician or physician group is extinguished as a practice model. Physicians are now employees of a hospital. As for hospitals, there are few stand-alone hospitals that operate independently. Hospitals are now part of large conglomerates, negotiating pricing with manufacturers and insurance companies. Profit-making has superseded patient care for many of these corporations. Nearly all medical equipment and drugs are sourced from group purchase organizations or GPOs that supply hospitals. These GPOs grew into powerful operations for the purpose of negotiating better prices for the hospital or hospital systems. Yet, prices have largely increased as these GPOs raise the fees they charge pharmaceutical companies and pass on only a partial discount to their member hospitals.

Recycling and cleaning equipment parts, instead of using disposable ones, became the standard in hospitals and clinics. And the aim of all these changes was to achieve a more efficient way of delivering health care equitably. Instead, medicine has become monetized, and we have produced some very well-paid hospital CEOs. Insurance companies are charging privately insured patients higher monthly payments, deductibles, and copays each year with less coverage and more restrictive drug formularies. Even the cost of generic drugs is exorbitant if they are not included in the insurer's formulary or list of approved drugs. Prior authorizations have become exhausting, and step therapy for chronic diseases has become a current way to delay the approval of newer, more expensive drugs. None of these changes have made health care cheaper or more equitable.

Additionally, while I have seen the explosion of technology use in medicine, from electronic health records to virtual medicine, telehealth, and data science, what I consistently read is that we have not improved patient outcomes or cost of care. The way my father used to practice medicine is remotely familiar to me in today's model of care.

Physical touch through proper examination is a powerful tool to connect a physician to the patient. Auscultation is the act of listening to the organs, like the heart, lungs, and intestines. Percussion is the active tapping of body parts, used to examine the size, borders, and consistency of the organs and whether fluid exists where it should not. By performing these exams to test the function of bones, the skin, and other parts of the body, physicians used to develop rapport with their patients, eventually earning their patient's trust. This type of interaction between doctors and their patients is fading away quickly, becoming a once-practiced, lost art of medicine, one that Dad learned early on in his career and practiced faithfully until he retired at eighty-four.

Dad knew his patients. He believed in the magic of eye contact and touch, taking the time to thoroughly examine his patients. A stethoscope was all he needed to listen to the heart and lungs. He would palpate the rest of the organs, carefully listening for abnormal sounds. A brilliant diagnostician, he paid attention to every detail, such as the patient's eyes, skin, nails, and bumps or bruises on the body. The family members present with the patient always had the opportunity to ask questions. Patients trusted my father implicitly and knew that he would recommend treatments and interventions that were in their best interest. The extent of intervention would be commensurate with the patient's and family's wishes. Because he took the time to know his patients, Dad knew what they would want, yet he would always present multiple options to ensure his patients made an informed decision.

Sometimes he would come home and call a friend with expertise in the area he was exploring for his patients, to be sure he had all the most current, up-to-date information. At times, he was so saddened by the diagnosis he had delivered to his patients that he would seek a period of solace by praying for the family. When patients passed in the hospital, he would immediately visit the family, surrounding their loved ones to console and comfort them. Patients were not a number or source of income to him. Dad was a true healer who was disappointed when terminal diseases impeded his efforts.

One of my fondest memories is spending time in Dad's office during school vacations. I would field phone calls, file charts, and check patients in and out as they came to see my father. Patients would wait in my dad's office for hours to see him. It seemed like at 1 p.m., everyone who had an appointment that afternoon would arrive at the same time, usually a half hour before the office even opened for the afternoon. They would eagerly sit in the small waiting room. Patients who had an appointment at 2 p.m. would arrive by 12:30 p.m. By 2:30, when Dad was already running a half hour late, they had been in the office for two hours already. That is when they would start to complain that the doctor was always running behind.

Sometimes there would be emergencies, keeping Dad at the hospital longer than any of us expected. The office technology was not as sophisticated as what is available now. There were no reminders sent to patients for appointments. Yet, patients rarely canceled their appointments. With no way to alert patients that the doctor was running late, we could only let patients know when they arrived at the office that their appointment would be later than expected. To this day, I am still not sure why patients who had come to see him for decades would come in early for their appointments. Perhaps they were hoping for a miracle that day, and he would be running ahead of schedule. Maybe someone in the appointment slot before them was not going to show up, and they would get lucky and see him earlier. Whatever their logic, it usually did not work out that way.

I will never forget their faces when they left the office. They were always smiling and carrying on about what a wonderful doctor my father was. It was as though they had been to church or experienced some sort of shaman healing. He had listened carefully and patiently to their complaints and focused on their physical well-being, emotional well-being, and their overall sense of happiness. By the time they left the office, there was a plan in place to ensure that they would have a better quality of life.

My father would order tests when necessary, prescribe medications when warranted, or refer patients to other specialists when appropriate. He had a circle of specialists whose expertise he trusted. His referrals to the specialists had nothing to do with whether those physicians were also in the patient's in-or-out of network or covered by the health plan. The experts he chose were the ones he would have chosen to treat his own family.

The daily routine for Dad was making rounds in the hospital in the morning to see his patients. He went to three different hospitals. During his very thorough visits with his patients at the hospitals, he would masterfully communicate with them, ensuring they felt seen and heard. Sometimes he would take me along with him on rounds. This was before HIPAA. He would always ask his patients if they minded that I was observing that day. When patients were not doing well or were immune compromised, I would patiently wait in the nurse's lounge for him to complete rounds. The lounge was often smoke-filled, with nurses puffing away at their cigarettes during their breaks. You would think that was the oddest scene, but frankly, seeing a patient smoke in their hospital room during rounds was the most shocking.

The nurses' uniforms were freshly pressed with matching crisp, white hats. The shape and color of the hats varied depending on whether they were student nurses or graduates. This was an extremely professional look. I realize that wearing dresses as uniforms with stockings and shoes may have been quite uncomfortable for the nurses in those days. Yet, their pleasant demeanor relayed the opposite. I do not recall ever hearing anyone complain about their uniforms as I waited in the lounges. It was uncommon to hear anyone complain about misbehavior, yelling, or inappropriateness in the hospital. Of course, I may have been too young to pay attention to or be privy to those types of conversations. As I understand it today, there are far fewer reports of conflicts between doctors and nurses in countries where traditional uniforms are still the norm.

There was something magical about the hospitals during those days. The environment was incredibly clean. The rooms were not beautiful, but they were spotless. There was not a lot of equipment in the hallways with hanging wires and attachments to trip people innocently walking by. I do recall a few orderlies and nurse's aides on each floor assisting the nursing staff. Most memorable, however, were the candy stripers and volunteers in the hospitals.

They would stand out as the people in red and white striped uniforms, with bright smiles, welcoming everyone and making sure they had directions to where they were going. These volunteers would visit patients with carts stocked with magazines, toys, and freshly knit blankets and throws donated by volunteers.

I was not cognizant of any friction when I walked into the hospitals back then. Quite the opposite, I observed a group of people working extremely hard to see to it that their patients improved. Circles of residents formed outside each patient's room. I could hear them enthusiastically discuss patient cases with their faculty member, often referring to note cards to refresh their memory on the information they had collected when they made rounds on the same patients earlier. Residents worked hard at building a great reputation with their mentors.

Unlike many doctors today, Dad was not limited by insurance companies on which tests he was able to order and when and where the patient needed to go for these tests. There was a greater level of freedom and choice in those days for doctors. I really do miss the days when doctors were independent and worked as solo docs or as a group, owning their own practice. They made decisions about their patients and what was best for them and rarely worried about getting approval from an insurance company.

Doctors could prescribe medication they thought would be best for their patients. Their decision was not based on a list of what the insurance company would cover or dependent on contracts with pharmaceutical manufacturers. Indeed, the doctors were truly quarterbacks with full decision-making power, driving the care for their own patients, both in and out of the hospital. There was a consistency of care that is largely absent today. This continuity allowed primary care and internal medicine physicians to work collaboratively with their patients, which was critical to my father's success with his patients.

For example, if my father knew that a patient would not be compliant with a medication that had to be taken four times a day, he would look for a similar medication that was twice daily, knowing the patient was more likely to be compliant. It was his way of individualizing patient care for the best possible outcome. When my dad counseled patients to stop smoking, and they refused, he would begin by asking them how many cigarettes they smoked each day. Then he would ask them how many they were willing to give up per day. They would usually opt for 3 to 5 cigarettes. My father would get a verbal agreement from them that when he saw them on their next visit, his expectation was that they would be smoking five cigarettes less per day. He negotiated with patients to optimize their health every day and used practical methods to achieve the best results. I do not have any statistics on how successful his method of counseling was, but I do recall speaking to numerous patients who claimed that my dad saved their life by helping them to quit smoking.

What I have come to realize is that my father instinctively applied what many leaders and life coaches recommend as steps to breaking unhealthy habits and developing positive ones instead. To get his patients to quit smoking, Dad created a vision of achieving a better health status, the ability to walk further without feeling out of breath, and being able to do more to enjoy life. He would then engage the patient to build a plan that would yield success by asking for what the patient thought to be a reasonable change. Dad followed up with the patient enthusiastically during future visits and reviewed their goals, celebrating any successful milestones. I was present during multiple discussions with his patients. Undeterred by a patient's failure, he continued to help them persevere. He was magical in influencing his patients to live healthier lives.

How was my father able to accomplish so much? I often wondered when I watched him interact with his patients. He was a patient man, never getting upset or angry with those who had failed to keep their end of the agreement.

Instead, he would start over with a more achievable goal. Always looking for wins for his patients, I would often hear him laughing loudly in celebration with those patients who had achieved their milestones of smoking cessation, abstinence from alcohol or drugs, or weight loss. He was a cardiologist with a primary interest in maintaining his patient's heart health. But he also knew he had to support their minds if he wanted to achieve sustainable results. My father was a healer of the mind, body, and soul.

Medicine was not perfect when he was in his mid-career. As a result, the government began to increase its involvement to address the gaps in medicine. They began to increase their involvement by enforcing new rules and regulations in the name of improving how medicine was being practiced, with the goal of creating a more equitable and efficient medical system.

Efficiency meant cutting down on the number of diagnostic tests and medical interventions. Insurance companies eagerly followed the same path as government payers. Arguably, the original intent was admirable, yet the outcome has been less than desirable. As the number of regulations and the need for prior authorizations grew, the need for more paperwork and more red tape grew steadily. Many doctors, regardless of where they practiced, spent hours filling out forms and checking boxes to complete the paperwork necessary for their patients to receive diagnostic tests and treatments. As the need to complete more paperwork increased, the patient-doctor relationship began to suffer.

Sadly, patients were on the receiving end of the reduced amount of time with their physicians. Doctors were quickly forced to give up forty-five-minute time slots with the patients, exchanging this for fifteen minutes just to keep up with the paperwork. Unfortunately, this change resulted in dissatisfaction for both patients and doctors with the way medicine was being practiced. While the income for physicians decreased substantially, their workload increased. Patients began to lose their ability to build trust with their physicians, and physicians became disenchanted with the practice of medicine. My father's way of doing things, just as with many other doctors, was being sacrificed in exchange for compliance with regulations that, at times, made no sense.

My father resisted the changes and spent the same amount of time with his patients while being forced to hire more help in the office to deal with the administrative burden of practice. More changes at the government level reduced reimbursement to hospitals for Medicare and Medicaid patients. Private insurers quickly followed suit. Hospitals had to act accordingly to sustain their existence. Physician assistants and nurse practitioners were hired to keep up with patient volume in a more cost-effective way. Physicians began to leave the field of medicine.

The administration staff of hospitals grew exponentially. To cut down on costs for hospitalized patients, committees were formed to consider various surgical equipment and medications to narrow the options. Instead of choosing treatments based on what is best for their individual patients, doctors have had to balance choosing effective, novel medications and their fiscal impact on the system where they are employed. What was meant to bring a set of balance and fairness to medical care resulted in more struggles for patients and an endless number of hoops for doctors to jump through.

Significant changes in medicine began prior to 2000, when I was just beginning my career after college, and I would ask Dad how things were going. I was considering going back to school to pursue a career in medicine. Though he would still say he loved the practice of medicine, Dad would often discuss the unnecessary number of calls to insurance companies to seek authorization for routine tests, which he used to order without any resistance in the past. Dad was a true patient advocate, never giving in to insurance companies that denied his patients tests he considered to be critical to their diagnosis and treatment.

Recalling one of his dear patients, he told me about a time when he ordered an MRI for a patient who had deteriorating eyesight, massive headaches, and dizziness, which were all recent symptoms. The insurance company denied the patient's MRI and requested an eye exam and a visit to a neurologist for migraines. My father knew his patients well. He knew whether they needed an eye exam or an MRI. The insurance companies do not typically have doctors who have practiced medicine reviewing these types of authorizations unless a case is escalated to a higher level. Instead, non-practitioners are often reviewing authorizations via algorithms that are set to deny, delay, or approve a request for a test.

Dad did not settle for the length of time it would take to appeal the denial for his patient, who needed an MRI. Instead, he sent the patient to the emergency room and had them order an MRI for the patient. The MRI was done, showing a tumor in the brain. The patient was operated on immediately, and the tumor was able to be removed since it had not attached itself to many of the surrounding tissues in the brain. It was a cancerous tumor. My father's swift actions saved his patient's life, but to save a life, he was forced to find a workaround due to the insurance company's lack of urgency.

Medicine has evolved even more now, making workarounds impossible. Insurance companies and so-called group purchase organizations are profiting every day and siphoning healthcare dollars into a black hole. In addition to the regulations, hospitals were mandated to create electronic health records, which are meant to streamline health care, be more accurate, and be more successful with billing. Yet, many of their own surgery centers or departments within the hospital have different electronic record systems that often do not communicate.

Doctors have had to continually adjust to new protocols and follow treatments mandated by these protocols and guidelines, with little opportunity to order other medications and individualize patient care. For example, to opt-out of a certain treatment set as default, providers must click multiple times to override the system. Incidentally, these protocols and guidelines are not always evidence based. Sometimes newly approved, branded products with better efficacy or tolerance are omitted strictly due to cost. Physicians often need to click 20 or 30 times before they get to the end of the patient record to complete all the necessary information. Therefore, job satisfaction is at its lowest for healthcare providers. This spells danger for all of us who will be patients at some point in our lives.

Nurses are also leaving their field in masses, leaving hospitals short-staffed and unable to manage patient loads. Thinking back to when I delivered my first child by cesarian section, I recall the nurses patiently reviewing information about how to care for my new child. I remember them coming to see me every morning to make sure I was successful in nursing and comfortable with changing and bathing the baby. Fast forward to today, and you will notice nurses rarely have time to educate or counsel their hospitalized patients. They are tethered to the computerized prescription order entry systems to ask for additional prescriptions and entry of patient information.

In many cases, they are burdened with more patients than they should be caring for at a time, and terrified of hurting a patient because of their limited time to ensure drugs are administered correctly or that they can get to a patient on time when a bed alarm goes off. Nurses are likely the most underpaid and overworked population in the medical community, based on my recent research and observations. When I review starting salaries for nurses compared to other starting salaries or entry-level positions, I am astonished by the disparity of pay compared to other professions. Nurses are constantly at the bedside. They understand the patient and recognize their needs, perhaps more than the rounding physicians, yet their voices are lost in the chaos of today's hospital systems.

As for patient care, it is sad to see how the increasing burden of administrative responsibilities to payers, which control reimbursement for services rendered, has driven physicians further away from their goals of excellent patient care. Physicians are vocal about these administrative obstacles and admit that they are responsible in large part for the loss of their independence. While physicians know how to provide excellent patient care, administrators, government regulators, insurance providers, and sometimes even the FDA has interfered with the process to the point that physicians and other providers are leaving the field of medicine in droves. Those who have stayed with their profession often experience burnout. Others have learned to put up with the challenges they face and choose the path of least resistance just to survive.

While insurance companies have enjoyed billions in profits, graduating doctors who go into the practice of medicine, owing thousands of dollars for their education, must sometimes work long hours and into their fifties just to pay off their school loans because of the exceedingly low insurance reimbursement rates, resulting in lower starting salaries. This is a reality that physicians face when they choose the field of medicine. It is unsettling to watch the number of healthcare administrators, who have nothing to do with actual patient care, grow year after year while the number of providers who care for patients is decreasing.

Among the many changes made in medicine, a new form of specialty emerged as part of the U.S. medical landscape. The goal for these doctors, known as hospitalists, was to play a crucial role in patient care at the hospital level. This group of doctors was born out of the need for specialists familiar with hospital medicine, as well as hospital policies and procedures. There are now over 40,000 such doctors in the U.S. Though the emergence of this specialty a decade and a half ago was originally thought to be an enhancement to patient care in the hospital, I am not so sure that this is the case. The connection to patients built over the years with a primary physician is no longer evident, often impacting the comfort level of the patients and their families while in the hospital setting.

When my father routinely saw his patients in the hospital, he knew his patients and their families well. Some of these families were patients for generations. More importantly, my father knew how to relay unwelcome news to each patient and anticipated their reaction based on the many years he had spent with them. He was acutely aware of cultural differences and how some families needed to be notified in case of diagnosis of a terminal illness.

In my father's case, he met his hospitalist physician for the first time as he was being informed about his diagnosis. The physician's assistant from the gastroenterology office, who assumed that no life-saving measures would be taken, appeared cold and lacking compassion when she followed up after the news was delivered. However, given the fact that she had never met my father either, the interaction became more of a transactional one. I wish my father had his own physician as his quarterback, just as he had done with his patients when he was a physician covering his patients' care in and out of the hospital, consulting with others to order tests and recommend treatments.

In today's model, outpatient physicians and hospitalists seldom communicate about the patient's hospitalization, so there is a disconnect between the hospital and a patient's primary physicians. This responsibility of care is left entirely to the hospitalist group. The outpatient physician, typically a primary care or internal medicine physician, is often unaware of a patient's hospitalization, particularly if the only way they are made aware is through one of the hundreds of emails that a physician receives. Otherwise, if the outpatient physician happens to check a patient's electronic record, they can view the course of hospitalization. If they do not look at that, they may not ever find out until the patient tells them.

This lack of communication leads to disjointed care of the patient. The outpatient physician may have much to offer about a patient's history and disposition, which can help the hospital physician, but the lack of connection means the hospitalist operates without that critical knowledge. Even if the outpatient physician has this history documented, it does not always mean the hospitalist has reviewed the full history included in the patient's record. Another concern is the follow-through of care once the patient is discharged. Primary physicians are out of the loop regarding what happened in the hospital, making it burdensome for them to follow through with the patient on any treatment plan created during their stay in the hospital. Hospitalists also have the disadvantage of having no previous relationship with the patient. They may be giving life-altering news to total strangers. How is effective patient engagement possible when the foundation of the relationship with a provider is flawed?

We face a precarious time in medicine with the many changes, a lack of significant improvement in healthcare outcomes or efficiencies, and the ongoing dissatisfaction of patients and providers alike. We are on the brink of a dangerous shortage of providers in the next decade and beyond.

Meanwhile, administrators at hospitals and insurance companies continue to enjoy hefty salaries, demanding elevated levels of productivity from providers while they restrict their ability to utilize state-of-the-art equipment and pharmaceutical products. It may be difficult to imagine that an administrator may control whether you receive an intravenous or oral equivalent of a drug as an inpatient in the hospital, or whether you receive a cheaper, generic antibiotic or a newer, targeted antibiotic for a specific bacterium.

Indeed, hospital administrators control drug and device budgets and limit their use to stay within their budgets. Pharmacists are in the undesirable position of having to implement these budgets by acting as gatekeepers of access to many new drugs and devices. Surgeons and anesthesiologists, who are responsible for a significant amount of patient care and contribute to the bottom line of the hospital's financials as a multi-disciplinary team, must advocate for newly approved products they would like to utilize. Yet, the decision-making power often lies with those who are indirectly involved with patient care or do not have the expertise to make decisions regarding the specific drug or device.

Adding to the frustration are government agencies, such as the Centers for Medicare and Medicaid Services (CMS), who have set quality metrics that providers and hospitals must meet for reimbursement. But how are providers to manage this if they are limited or restricted in their access to the medications or medical devices and equipment that would enable them to improve outcomes?

There is growing friction between the decision makers or gatekeepers and front-line providers asking for treatments they consider to be best for a patient. Providers must follow a long and arduous process to ask for the addition of a drug or device. Busy schedules and competing demands on their time make it nearly impossible to successfully complete this process, which favors the "nay-sayer" administrators. Sadly, this becomes a game of endurance and persistence. It is simply impossible for practitioners to fight on several fronts at the same time. When a patient is hospitalized, a provider may be fighting insurance companies for outpatient treatments for a patient and fighting the hospital administration to gain access to treatments that may be restricted only under exceptional circumstances or unavailable altogether at the hospital.

The interactions during the initial hospitalization were only the beginning of our journey and lessons learned. Things changed when Dad became the patient. We needed to help Dad pack his own healthcare parachute as he was now the patient, entering an unrecognizable and troubled medical environment. With all these challenges, you might be wondering how you could navigate the current healthcare system if you were faced with a medical crisis such as the one we faced. Our family was more prepared than most, yet we still struggled. Throughout the next chapter, I will share some of the lessons we gleaned during our experiences in hopes of sparing other families from the pain we endured. Having the presence of mind and the ability to discuss options with a knowledgeable neutral party, such as a patient advocate or concierge medicine physician, may be one option to preserve family relationships during a difficult and emotional journey of a loved one's terminal illness through the current healthcare system.

Chapter 9

Reflections: Pack Your Own Healthcare Parachute

"Pack your own parachute" is a term I heard many years ago from one of my managers at the first company I joined after college, referring to one's career. And now, this term applies just as much to being your own advocate as a patient. As discussed in Chapter 8, doctors have extraordinarily little incentive or time to fight for their patients and their needs. Providers are consistently trying to do the right thing, yet the inertia of the system that is set up in and out of the hospital today trips them up every step of the way. Until systems begin to allow doctors to have the authority and autonomy they need to care for their patients, it is up to the individual patient or their advocate to do their research, ask questions, and seek outside expert advice to determine the best path forward when facing a terminal diagnosis. In Dad's case, what I never expected was the shift in family dynamics after his diagnosis. This experience was the first of many lessons.

Never underestimate the power of destiny over your carefully crafted plans. And be grateful for life today because, tomorrow, life can exist in a completely different form, if at all. A simple yet extraordinary concept of gratitude is central to one's existence and well-being. Yet, it is a rare practice in our society. The wanting for more wealth, more material, more fame, and more recognition drives us each day until we are brimming with burnout. Distracted by the everyday bustle, we often overlook the importance of time with family. So, what is it that you can do today to reset your mind to be more grateful and live in the present rather than chase the future? The future with our father never arrived for our family. We were ready to begin enjoying Dad, version 2.0, a relaxed and retired doctor with a new mission of relishing his free time and traveling to visit his grandchildren around the country. But God had a different plan for us.

Resilience and Mindfulness

Life is precious, and everything we have is a gift to be thankful for in our lives. Mindfulness and gratitude are critical to building resilience. Practicing mindfulness is paramount to being prepared if life suddenly unravels before you. For us, the unraveling came with news about Dad's cancer diagnosis. Having the presence of mind to quickly process information, accept a new norm, and act quickly is critical during a health emergency. Emerging data continue to demonstrate the improvement of outcomes in patients who practice mindfulness. Imagine a world where the practice of mindfulness and meditation is accessible by and offered to all patients. If this were the case, we might need fewer anti-anxiety drugs, fewer sleep aids, and even fewer painkillers. Would the practice of mindfulness and meditation in patients with a terminal illness, along with conventional medical treatment, help reduce the anxiety patients face? We clearly do not have the answers, and sadly, there is not enough funding for these practices to be assessed in studies. To be a bit cynical as someone who has been involved in introducing multiple drugs to the medical community, if mindfulness and meditation were reimbursable or packaged in a vial, we would see a lot more funding for these practices.

It is essential to study and eventually recognize these practices as a component of a multi-pronged approach to conventional treatment. The first time I was introduced to mindfulness practice was during my graduate studies. I found this practice not only extremely therapeutic but a necessary part of my daily routine. There were days when waking to face another day, one that would bring us closer to the end of my father's life, became unbearable. On the days when the gloomy, dark, and cold Rochester weather matched our mood after we dove into the most recent blood tests and scans, I clung to the practice of mindfulness like a lifeline.

My father fought valiantly for months; he did not want to fail, and he did not want to let us see him be defeated. His was a fight for the family, and it is agonizing to think he may have endured some of the interventions simply because he did not want to disappoint us.

Mindfulness and gratitude helped me focus on the beautiful life rather than being buried in the anguish of the loss of my father. What I came to appreciate was that my father entered this Earth for a calling. His calling was to heal others. And he completed that which he was summoned to do. He was blessed with eighty-five years of a life filled with challenges, all of which he overcame, except for the one that would end that beautiful life. Living close enough to be able to visit often and spend time with him during the final weeks and months was another source of inner peace. Your loved ones may not want to burden you by asking you to be around them. Yet, their spirit will be lifted each time they see family and friends. Be available and present to spend time with your loved ones during their most vulnerable moments. Your presence will give them the spiritual and emotional support they need to carry on. Be there for your loved ones and understand that what they want during their final days may be contrary to what you think. Presence is an inestimably precious gift.

Acceptance and Taking Time to Grieve

A Swiss-American psychiatrist first introduced the concept of the grieving process in her book, *On Death and Dying*. Elizabeth Kübler-Ross described what a patient diagnosed with a terminal illness may go through to finally come to terms with illness and death. The original five stages begin with denial, anger, depression, bargaining, and acceptance. It has since evolved to include seven stages that apply both to patients and families.

Acceptance of impending death is one of the most difficult concepts to reconcile. As such, it is the very last stage of the grieving experience. Some may believe that acceptance is the same as acquiescing or giving up. Acceptance is not giving up. One can remain hopeful and fight for a better outcome while remaining aware of the unavoidable in the case of a dear family member's terminal diagnosis. Acceptance is fighting as hard as you can for life and knowing that you will have to settle for what destiny brings.

Weaving between the stages during a grieving process, undulating back and forth with each emerging piece of information, is quite normal. Sometimes acceptance is flatly denied by both patients and their loved ones. At the beginning of his diagnosis, we were blinded by our vision of my father as an invincible man. After all, he was healthy, enjoying his life to the fullest every day. It seemed impossible that he would not be able to overcome the challenges presented by cancer, despite his age. Dad had just been dancing with us at a Persian New Year's celebration, and swimming with the stingrays, and snorkeling in the Cayman Islands two years ago. To say that we were in utter shock with his diagnosis is an understatement. Time was needed to process the information and accept it on our own terms.

For me, gaining more knowledge about Dad's cancer, the lack of effectiveness of available treatments, and the uncertainty around the harm of chemotherapy quickly pushed me into the bargaining and acceptance stage. It was unbearable to see Dad deteriorate. And his condition trapped my older sister in the anger and depression phase, never letting her progress to the final phase of acceptance. I am not an expert in the grieving process. However, this was my observation as I watched her suffer. Not surprisingly, I was asked by some of the providers whether my sister realized Dad was extremely ill and dying. This question was like pouring acid on a wound, leaving me feeling helpless since there was nothing I could do or say to help her.

I loved my sister and was frustrated with what our relationship had become. But at the same time, I knew she was suffering. Her family was incredibly supportive, surrounding her and accompanying her when she came to visit my father. The isolation I experienced during this time was overpowering. My children were always there for me, but the fear of overwhelming them kept me from sharing all that was happening.

Work was my only escape and where I could go to detangle myself from the reality of my personal crisis. I had the flexibility to work remotely with limited travel due to budgetary concerns at the time. Still, it was not fair to my employees or my peers to be distracted by my own personal tragedy. When the phone rang, and it was one of my managers needing to discuss challenges, I had a difficult time empathizing with their world. The calamity I was facing made it difficult for me to be a good leader. I had never felt more distraught with the way I let my team down during Dad's illness, and I beat myself up over it for months. Taking time off to focus on my own well-being as I was caring for my father and dealing with family issues would have been a better decision.

During the research for this book, I had numerous conversations with families who have had similar experiences, wishing they had been warned about the pitfalls of dealing with a terminal illness of a family member. It is natural to want to do everything humanly possible to beat the odds. We all feel certain that with a strong will to live, coupled with modern medicine, cancer can be overcome. In so many cases, this is true. We celebrate when we see pictures of people finishing their last round of chemo or other cancer treatments, declaring their victory over cancer. Sadly, this is not always the outcome. While hope is critical, denial is destructive and insidious, like a cancer that slowly ravages the soul and cripples the mind.

Offering a Hand

People wanted to help me during this challenging time, but they did not always know how to do that. Often, the best thing that we can do for others is to be there for them to cry with, to talk about their loved one, or simply to provide a hug or other emotional support. Being patient, compassionate, and empathic is critical to the process of grieving, whether you are the one grieving or supporting a family member or friend. This was something I needed to remember with my grieving sister from the start. My failure to be patient and compassionate and to show empathy for what she was feeling was the beginning of the demise of our sisterhood.

Compassion

For some of us in the family, the grieving process began immediately after the failed surgery. For others, the unsuccessful surgery only fed the desire to continue wishing for miracles through interventions. Having compassion for other family members with differing opinions became impossible for me. I was already in the negotiation phase of the grieving process, hoping for less suffering and praying for quality of life for however long Dad was going to be with us.

Our individual approach to processing information separated us immediately after Dad's surgery. What began as a harmless but necessary process of selecting a proxy, morphed into a destructive weapon to drive decisions on various interventions without the family's consensus. Dad went along with many of these interventions enthusiastically at first but began refusing them when he realized that they were causing him more discomfort and distress. Observing this dynamic broke my heart as I witnessed my father growing weaker and weaker after each invasive procedure. I cried alone, disappointed in my inability to stop the powerful train fueled by the conductor's denial, anger, and despair. My mom tried to slow the train down. My sister, the conductor, continued to push forward, convinced of her ability to create a miracle.

The medical staff could feel the friction between the family members from three floors away while my father was hospitalized, at one point advising the resolution of issues that existed between us. "Your father will be leaving you all, but you all will be here and need to carry on as a family. I am sure he would want the family to remain intact," was the compelling advice from one of the nurse practitioners during Dad's final days.

Healthcare Proxy

Choosing a healthcare proxy involves several factors. First, it is imperative that the proxy's emotional connection to the patient does not impede their ability to make decisions. This can be difficult, especially if they know your wishes but personally do not agree with them. Second, a question that needs to be answered is whether the designated proxy can comfortably talk with medical staff and doctors. Are they able to ask for clarification if they do not understand something? Finally, in some cases, a proxy is meant to serve as the family's spokesperson to ease some of the burdens of providers having to interact with multiple family members, explaining the same information over and over. Will the proxy represent decisions made by the family, or will they make decisions unilaterally based on what they think to be the best path forward?

There is such a thing as choosing the wrong proxy. What if the proxy is recommending options that the family and the medical team disagree with? Will they move forward with the family's decision, even if they do not agree with it? Without critical measures being put into place, these situations can end up causing more division and make a challenging situation even more complicated.

When it came to our family, we did not have a clear discussion on how Dad's wishes would be communicated through my sister. We were not a family that openly discussed serious illness or situations where important decisions about resuscitation and intubation would have to be made. The medical staff was acutely aware of the family's disagreements about the best path forward, often having to tiptoe around sensitive discussions, such as life-saving measures. Clarity is essential in sensitive situations, especially when choosing a healthcare proxy. In addition to the individual not being impeded by their feelings for the patient, the proxy should ideally consult with the family prior to any decision-making, or at least this is the way my mother had imagined the proxy to work for my father.

Research

Beating the odds in cancer is dependent on so many factors. For us, this was one of the most difficult lessons. The type of cancer, the extent of disease or staging, available treatments, age at diagnosis, mental and physical health, and resilience all play a significant role in one's prognosis. However, another important and often overlooked factor is the experience of the healthcare facility and the expertise of its faculty members with the type of cancer.

Not all medical centers are created equal, and outcomes for patients can be quite variable. For example, for cholangiocarcinoma, Memorial Sloan

Kettering, Mayo Clinic, and MD Anderson are the highest-rated centers. Specialists at these centers have expertise in treating this type of cancer, conduct multiple clinical trials, and have ancillary clinical staff capable of managing treatment-related adverse events and complications of disease progression.

While not all patients and families have access to the top hospitals in the country, most do have the ability to engage virtually with specialists around the country. Since my father's illness, I have become a passionate supporter of comprehensive research to identify best-performing hospitals and doctors and recommend others engage one to three additional specialists to review their medical case prior to making any final treatment decisions.

The availability of telehealth and electronic health records provides a quick method of sharing medical records and test results with specialists all over the country. Seeking at least a second opinion and perhaps a third opinion in complex cases may delay the time to care. In return, the time spent speaking with several specialists may clarify the path forward for the family and result in consensus regarding treatment options. Occasionally, patients voice concerns about offending their physician by getting a second opinion. Confident, capable physicians should never get offended about a patient making an informed decision about their health and seeking other expert opinions.

Patient Advocacy

We were continuously advocating for my father during his hospitalizations and outpatient visits. The physicians and other healthcare providers were always gracious about answering all our questions. Streamlining the flow of information by having one objective patient advocate or a concierge physician may have been more helpful in our case. We often interpreted the information we received based on our own tinted lenses.

The role of such an advocate would be to help the family focus on established health goals and assist with decisions. The patient advocate or concierge medicine provider will ensure that the patient and family's wishes are adhered to, both in and out of the hospital. They will also be a reliable source of information and able to expand upon or clarify topics that may be too complex for the layperson to comprehend.

Another advantage of a concierge medicine provider is their ability to have access to the patient's medical records and close the gap of communication between inpatient and outpatient providers. A concierge medicine provider or patient advocate should be independent, without financial ties to hospital systems, releasing them from any obligation to recommend one treatment over another. Patient advocates may also get involved when families have complex decisions to make, ensuring the patient's well-being and avoidance of harm are prioritized.

The climb back from the surgery for Dad was like watching an injured hiker struggle with a climb on Kilimanjaro. It was difficult to watch, and there was little we could do to assist. With a myopic focus on the quantity of life, we lost sight of Dad's quality of life. If we had a do-over, I am not sure Dad would have wanted even the initial intervention, knowing the difficulties of recovery and lack of functional reserve to return to baseline. What haunts me every day is whether interventions hurt Dad by shortening his life in the end. Sadly, I will never know the answer to this question.

Cancer and the Elderly

The biggest hurdle for Dad from the start was his age. The double whammy of cancer and older age makes the elderly population more vulnerable to treatment-related adverse events. The risk of adverse events must be weighed heavily against any benefit of the intervention. Invasive interventions, when performed on elderly patients, often do more harm than good. The more interventions that are performed, the higher the risk for complications, either during the procedure or recovery. A vast majority of clinical trials performed to evaluate the efficacy and safety of cancer treatments omit elderly patients, making it exceedingly difficult to extrapolate the results of cancer treatment trials to include the elderly. How do multiple comorbidities impact the effect of these treatments on the elderly? These are important questions that remain unanswered in this population.

I recall our family meeting with the medical oncologist and his fellow well. It was a painful meeting, with Dad already looking frail after his open abdominal surgery and three procedures, all requiring anesthesia in less than a month. It is likely Dad had not yet fully recovered from all the anesthesia and post-surgical complications when we met with the medical oncologist team.

Repeated doses of anesthetics alone can impact the mind of the elderly patient, even without the existing cancer and compromised immune system. This is due to the inability of older individuals to metabolize drugs as quickly as their younger cohorts, making a recovery more difficult. Baseline mental status and other comorbidities can also affect outcomes post-procedure or surgery. Some of the complications from anesthesia include immediate postoperative delirium, which may lead to postoperative cognitive dysfunction lasting weeks, months, or longer. One of the most terrifying experiences for families is witnessing significant changes in the mental status of their loved ones after surgery. I have heard numerous families wishing their mom or dad still had that "bum knee," which was better than having a parent who has a knee that works well but a brain that fails them daily after having gone through surgery.

It is critical, therefore, to ask that an anesthesiologist specializing in the elderly or geriatric population manage the anesthesia for your loved one. Geriatric specialists may be able to avoid certain drugs that are implicated in causing mental status changes in the elderly. It is also prudent to ask for a pre-surgical cognitive test to be performed to assess mental status and function, thus establishing a baseline. A post-surgical test can then measure functional gaps after the surgery to aid in building a recovery plan.

Fortunately, considerable progress has been made to minimize patient harm by evaluating older patients to predict how they may tolerate cancer treatments. "First Do No Harm" is particularly fitting for older patients. The National Comprehensive Cancer Network (NCCN) has developed guidelines to optimize patient outcomes by reducing harm from toxicities or complications of treatment and balancing them with quality-of-life factors.

These guidelines, driven by the Comprehensive Geriatric Assessment (CGA), screen patients for treatment. CGA takes three factors into consideration to optimize individual care. The first is functional status, or the ability of an elderly patient to perform daily functional tasks, such as bathing, dressing, toileting, and eating independently. Functional status is predictive of outcomes in the elderly population. Another factor is the degree of polypharmacy, or the number of medications prescribed for the patient. And finally, the number of comorbid conditions is considered.

Once CGA has been performed, the goals of treatment, such as survival, cure, remission, or palliation of symptoms, are also carefully considered in the context of the assessment results. Ideally, a geriatric oncology team should meet with the family at the time of diagnosis to discuss all these factors prior to deciding on the next steps. There will be changes to the assessment with each intervention; therefore, it is important to re-assess with each additional intervention to determine if the current course is still appropriate for the patient.

When I think back to the family gathered around in a small room, our eyes open wide, hanging on to every word we heard during his oncology visit, my heart begins to ache all over again. The mind is a powerful machine. When one has a preconceived notion, and information that will support that notion, thoughts and beliefs will be selectively stored in the memory. While some of the warnings were clearly renumerated, the family cheered Dad on for chemo, a double-edged sword that can cause significant harm.

During this meeting, Dad had a challenging time describing his cancer. Perhaps it was denial, or he was simply confused, which should have been a flag against more toxic treatments. He was noticeably quiet during the meeting, speaking only when he was directly questioned by the fellow or the attending. One statement Dad made during that meeting was the first clue we all missed. Dad made a point to confirm that the chemo he would start on would be an extremely low dose and separated by one week to allow him to recover from the treatment. He knew the dangers of chemotherapy and spoke up to remind the doctors to start the dose of his chemotherapy "low" and to go "slow."

It was not surprising that Dad's health deteriorated exponentially after each intervention. Later, as we contemplated each procedure, the lines between palliative, necessary, and excessive care became blurry. What I learned from this experience was that those hours, days, or weeks gained through multiple interventions may not be worth the pain and agony we put our loved ones through, particularly with aggressive cancers like my father's.

For our family, the geriatric consult for a thorough evaluation of Dad's overall status was recommended well into Dad's illness and chemo. This evaluation showed him to be at an increased risk of complications of severe side effects. In fact, he was 89% likely to experience severe side effects with chemotherapy. Sadly, this evaluation was only done to recommend the discontinuation of Dad's chemo after he experienced what the experts called chemo-induced delirium. My father was hospitalized in early November after receiving three courses of chemo. This time his admission was due to acute delirium. It was heartbreaking to see him struggle to answer simple questions, such as his age.

This was a man who recited Rumi poems from memory. This was a man who knew every detail about his patients, their ailments, and their medications. This was a man who knew every patient's loved one's names. This was not the man we once knew. When asked how old he was, he would smile and claim he was 125 years old. The first time I heard his response, I thought he was using his charming sense of humor. But as he repeated it, I knew there was something terribly wrong. I grew silent, as depression took over. Still grateful for his time with us, we began to joke around and accept the new norm with Dad. He had good days and bad days. We cherished the time we had together regardless of his mental status.

Hospital Systems

Hospitals are being run by corporations, which are focused on optimizing reimbursement. For example, when a patient is discharged earlier than expected, the payment for that patient's hospitalization from insurance or Medicare/Medicaid will likely be optimal. As soon as a patient enters the hospital, decisions are made about their treatment in terms of how they can manage outcomes while minimizing costs. One way to minimize costs is to discharge patients according to the reimbursement structure. If discharging a patient on day three of hospitalization vs. day four after knee surgery is more profitable according to the reimbursement structure for the hospital, then nearly all patients will be discharged on day three. To prevent patients from getting discharged too quickly, the Centers for Medicare and Medicaid have had to provide guardrails and implement practices that punish hospitals for readmission within a certain period after discharge by reducing hospital reimbursement rates or introducing fines for complications. This rule only applies to certain chronic conditions and patients recovering from specific surgeries and is not widely applied to the general hospitalized population.

Additionally, some medications and services utilized in the hospital are reimbursed, while others are not. Some procedures are more profitable when performed in surgery centers vs. the hospital. Equipment, such as robots used for surgery, can be very costly. The use of areas, such as the operating room, is also extremely expensive. Efficiency becomes the priority at hospitals, especially in acute care areas. These are just a few examples of hospital financial considerations when a patient is admitted. Until about twenty years ago, if there were complications, keeping the patients hospitalized longer, the coding system allowed the hospital to charge for all services provided, whether the complications were the result of negligence or not. The rules have changed since safety and quality initiatives were introduced into the hospitals. Additionally, with the affordable care act, bundled payments for specialty services were introduced. Bundled payments shift the risk of complications to the hospital and providers. Unfortunately, while the providers are taking on additional risk with the new payment policies, they are not afforded the autonomy to make many of the decisions.

Although doctors are the experts on what would benefit their patients, hospital regulations and the agenda that is focused on profitability tends to override individual physician-driven treatment decisions. Surprisingly, medications make up less than 1% of the total cost of care in hospitalized patients. Yet, hospitals are constantly focused on controlling drug costs. Even though pharmacists are trained to work on drug-drug interactions, reconciliation of controlled drugs, counseling patients at discharge about compliance with medications, etc., they are distracted by aggressive management of drug acquisition costs.

The hospital system pharmacist is often burdened with a silo budget that has nothing to do with patient outcomes, patient experience, or quality of care. They are incentivized to keep costs down, and that often translates into being forced to recommend inexpensive substitutes for newer FDA-approved drugs. Physicians often face a situation where they cannot get approval for the medication that they believe would provide the best outcome for their patients. FDA-approved drugs are often dismissed for unapproved substitutes simply to save money, even if better outcomes can be achieved for the patient with FDA-approved drugs. Why would that be the case? One explanation may be our complicated healthcare insurance system.

Astonishingly high rates of complications caused by medical errors, such as infections, oversedation, and falls, cause considerable loss due to reduced reimbursement or penalties. These complications contribute to exceedingly excessive costs of care and loss of profitability by hospitals. Yet, hospitals are slow to realize a strategy that reduces error, protects patients, and reduces costs.

Throughout my father's hospitalizations in the seven-month period of his illness, we met multiple doctors in multiple specialties. Ironically, the constant that we were grateful for during this emotional time was the group of hospitalists who rounded on the oncology floor and had come to know my father and his case well. One of the hospitalists stood out. He was young, kind, and passionate about patient care. Despite the existing hospital bureaucracy, our hospitalist was able to get some of the medications that Dad needed, but only after hours of phone calls and repeated requests. This is a daunting task for any provider. And the hospitalist may have settled for what the pharmacy recommended had it not been for us advocating for these medications throughout my father's hospitalizations. It quickly becomes exhausting for both the doctor and the patient.

We witnessed constant micromanaging across the hospital silos, impacting my father's care. Physicians and other providers are tasked with meeting quality and safety metrics as well as discharge timelines, while the pharmacy is charged with limiting their expenses. Today, hospitals remain operational in silos. Better outcomes could cost the hospitals much less, but silos prevent departments from taking a team approach to patient care. These silos have created an environment of friction, one that does little to foster collaboration.

It is nearly impossible to know about this issue unless you are well-embedded in the healthcare system or have a tremendous amount of experience with healthcare advocacy. In fact, this is an ugly secret no provider wants to share with hospital patients or their families.

Medical Error and Patient Harm

If the comprehensive geriatric assessment had been done, showing a near 90% risk of severe adverse events with chemotherapy, would my father have chosen this treatment? Though one can never be 100% sure that Dad's acute delirium, which caused yet another hospitalization, was related to the chemo, most experts at the hospital agreed that it was the probable cause, especially since no other source was identified as the culprit. During the discussion about

Dad's initiation of chemotherapy, I was listening to the facts shared with us about the potential harm, in return for the mere possibility of gaining an extra three months with a potentially worse quality of life. But I wanted to hear that the chemo would be more effective for Dad. And, of course, we would manage any adverse events with the use of other drugs. A patient advocate or a concierge physician looking solely at the patient's best interests may have had a different view of trying chemo.

In Dad's case, the patient harm caused by the chemo is not nearly as clear or glaring an error as wrong-side surgery or leaving an instrument in a patient after surgery. There have been other notable changes in the aim of reducing patient harm. It has been nearly three decades since Don Berwick, MD, a pediatrician, and a graduate of Harvard Medical School, set out to explore the improvement of health care and founded the Institute for Healthcare Improvement in the early 1990s.

Dr. Berwick's mission produced the first ever "To Err Is Human," an astounding report where it was revealed that nearly 100,000 patients die each year in our medical system due to preventable medical errors. Alarmingly high numbers of patients continue to be harmed by medical errors today. More recently, data was published in the British Medical Journal, where Johns Hopkins examined an eight-year period of data, showing medical errors as the cause of death in more than 250,000 patients in the U.S. each year. This number is equivalent to a large plane crashing and killing the passengers on board every single day. According to experts like Dr. Marty Makary, MD, MPH of Johns Hopkins, this figure is likely an underestimation of the reported numbers since death certificates do not capture details of medical errors. Dr. Makary points to a faulty medical billing system that lacks the ability to document medical errors because it was originally designed for billing rather than capturing health statistics. There are, however, other established surrogates of quality of care that are helpful in comparing individual hospital outcomes in this regard.

Dr. Berwick describes five specific dimensions to which all patients are entitled when in need of health care. The first of these, not surprisingly, is "Don't kill me" (no needless death), referencing any inappropriate treatment or negligence that may cause loss of life. Respiratory depression due to overutilization of narcotics is one such example. Thousands of patients die each year due to a lack of monitoring after being given narcotics in the hospital. Thankfully, there are a lot of developments around patient monitoring and a non-opioid approach to pain management, which will hopefully lead to a reduction in patient harm.

The second dimension is "Do help me; don't hurt me" (no needless pain). When I think back to how many times my father was poked with needles to measure his glucose levels, only to give him the most minute dose of insulin, I get sick to my stomach. He must have been poked thousands of times. While he could have continued his long-acting medications to keep his glucose levels manageable, the hospital-mandated practice for glucose management would not allow for this. Therefore, glucose checks every few hours became nearly impossible to endure. Near the end of his life, he would simply reject the test and/or insulin. I cannot imagine how the stress of being poked and the labor-intensive nature of the glucose checks can possibly improve outcomes. Why are hospitals not utilizing devices that use one stick and measure glucose at all time points during the day? The likely answer is cost. Where is the data to support the current standard?

Making one feel helpless in a hospital is the next dimension Dr. Berwick refers to: "Don't make me feel helpless" and "Don't keep me waiting." The helplessness that Dad experienced was the worst to witness. And the suffering that came with waiting for medications or procedures was distressing to see. All patients should have their dignity respected to the very end. Dying with dignity, to me, means doing everything to ensure a patient is not helpless at the end of life. My father was no exception.

And finally, Dr. Berwick urges hospitals, "Don't waste resources—mine or anyone else's." There are a lot of wasted resources in hospitals, involving both patients and providers. Time is the biggest source of waste with electronic health systems that are already too archaic or fail to address the system's practical needs. Electronic health records and computerized prescribing order entry systems can be impediments to quality care, yet they were designed to streamline care. Watching nurses and doctors click through multiple screens to get to a piece of information was distressing. They were clearly fatigued by the end of the day, creating a perfect setting for medical errors.

Timely, reliable, equitable, and safe health care is an existential necessity in our society. Today, doctors are encumbered by countless challenges that exist, limiting them to surviving in medicine rather than thriving in medicine. My hope is to inspire those who are the leaders in medicine to become disruptors of the status quo and change the way medicine is practiced today, so that no patient dies or is harmed due to medical error or suffers from pain when it is manageable, and that no patient is neglected or left helpless, and that resources are not wasted but rather utilized to foster cooperation and improvement of outcomes within hospital systems.

Chapter 10

End of a Precious Life

Time stood still, and with eyes that could see no further, I glanced at Dad once again. I clutched onto the cold sheet covering his arm, now wet with my tears. I laid my head on Dad's arm and imagined what it would be like if we were still a close family. Our family dynamic had taken on a new face since my father's diagnosis seven months ago. Dad was the glue that kept our family together. Cancer had eaten away at everything that we cherished about being a family unit. As Dad neared the end, a dark cloud of sorrow descended over the family, waiting to touch down. An emotional windstorm of anger, sadness, and fear took over each time there was an interaction between my older sister and me. We had come unglued.

Despite Dad's deteriorating condition, it was hard for her to see what we all had realized was happening. Dad was becoming progressively worse, and there was nothing that the doctors could do to save him. Whether or not to resuscitate Dad became a highly contentious topic. I tried to ignore these intrusive memories of days past and focus on Dad. "Dad," I started to whisper in desperation, "I am so sorry about what has happened. Everything will be okay. We know how much you endured so that you could stay with us. We all love you so much." I kissed his arm and squeezed his hand while he remained motionless.

My thoughts invaded again. When Dad was first diagnosed, he was determined to fight for his life and try everything possible to improve his survival. Somewhere along the way, fighting for his life changed to fighting to stay alive for his family. He was agreeable to nearly every intervention. The only time I saw him refusing an intervention was a few days ago when he gently told my older sister that he would think about the suggested procedure to remove the infection from his liver. That was the same day he declared to Mom that he would be leaving this world soon.

Mom had been at my father's side from the beginning of this journey and knew better than any of us what he would want. Often by his side, she would hear him advising friends and family on this topic when they were facing the question of resuscitation. "Why make them suffer more?" was his practical question when it came to resuscitation in the context of an end-stage terminal illness. In his opinion, resuscitation, in this instance, was going against the Hippocratic oath, a physician's pledge to avoid any treatment or procedure that may cause harm. Mom realized Dad's wishes when he confided in her. To my surprise, she was determined to take back decision-making power about my dad's care. Afterall, she was his power of attorney.

Reliving what happened in the past few days as I watched my father transition to an afterlife was like pouring acid into a wound. My mother was suffering in multiple ways during Dad's illness. Dad's horrific cancer, her sleepless nights, lack of food, anxiety, sorrow surrounding the immediate future, and, worst of all, seeing her daughters destroy their friendship over their father's illness had taken a toll on her physically. Mentally, she had grown even stronger and more deliberate than ever, knowing that she needed to respect her husband's wishes. Her daughters were taking on the burden of trying to decide the best way forward for their beloved Dad. Mom did not want any of us to be burdened with whether we had made the right decision regarding Dad's final days. Instead of allowing this situation to continue, she took charge.

Mom knew Dad would not want to be resuscitated if he stopped breathing or his heart stopped—not at this point of his illness. He had decided it was time to leave us. Mom followed his wishes, though this made her very uneasy. Up to this point, my sister had been Dad's proxy, relaying decisions to the medical team. When Mom stepped up, it was challenging for all of us to accept that our input was no longer needed. I can imagine this was especially difficult for my sister, who must have felt as if Mom was telling her that her role was no longer required. This change of guard may have contributed to her feelings of betrayal, isolation, and resentment, intermingled with her personal grief of losing Dad. I kissed Dad's hand again as I stood up slowly to walk around his bed to give mom a hug and wipe the tears running down her face. She laid her head on my shoulder for a moment. "Thank you, Mom, for all you have done for Dad. He loves you so much." Deep in thought, she turned her attention back to Dad, looking at him with adoration and deep love.

I walked around and sank into the chair next to Dad, taking his hand in mine. It felt cold and lifeless. Suddenly, I was reminded of my relationship with my sister, now on life support. When I was around my sister, it felt like we were both geared up for battle instead of uniting to make Dad's last few days as peaceful as possible. To apologize was out of the question, as we both believed we had been wronged by the other. We drew our battle lines, and our families had no choice but to back their leader. At a time when we needed to lean on each other, there was isolation, resentment, and anger festering and breeding a massive infection of its own. I have played the tape of the final few days, in my head over and over to this day, and I wish I could press delete and edit it like a bad scene in a movie.

Sadly, the memories of our exchanges were chiseled in my brain. When Dad realized he was quite ill, he insisted that we stay with him longer, if possible, when we visited, and he was sad when we left to go to our respective states of residence. His eyes would well up with tears as though to say, "I'm not sure I will be here when you return." I only know the unspoken words now, far better than I did during his illness. Much of the stress he experienced was concern over who would take care of Mom. He also worried about his grandchildren and their financial well-being. And above all, he wanted to see peace among us.

I smiled, thinking of a story Dad had shared with us in a moment of lucidity. It was about an exchange he had with a classmate who had been unkind. In an angry tone, he had let the young man know that he was terribly upset with him, admitting to us that he was immediately sorry about his behavior. The experience guided him to set his own ground rules for the rest of his adult life. Smiling as his eyes traveled to each of us surrounding his hospital bed, he struggled to get the words out. "Always say you are sorry first, make more friends than enemies, and love all humankind." Dad was a man who wanted nothing but peace and kindness in his life, yet he was about to leave us amid a stormy and hateful negative energy that was palpable in the room. It was clear he was determined to stay alive to see our differences resolved. Dad tried his best to fight death to the very end, but clearly being exhausted and defeated by the infectious state, he began to transition.

I began to sob, remembering the last moments I spent with Dad when he was still responding to us. Dad's love of food continued until Saturday, just days prior to him going into a deep sleep. Weakening by the hour, Dad was only able to move his head up and down if he wanted to eat what was offered. I recall my son Daniel and my daughter Alexandra being next to me in the room. We were on a scheduled visitation with Dad since the tension in our family would not allow for all of us to be around at the same time. When Daniel and Alex entered the room that morning just after I got there, he opened his eyes and lit up with a smile as though their presence had instantly supplied him with a boost of energy.

He closed his eyes just moments later, and when I offered him some of his favorite vanilla yogurt, he moved his chin up and down slowly. I fed him with a tiny spoon and could see him savoring each spoonful. Swallowing was difficult, yet he managed it slowly, determined to build up the energy he would need over the next few days. Watching him finish the serving with enjoyment is one of the last times I recall smiling during his final days with us. He opened his eyes once more that day when his grandson, affectionately known as "little Papa," walked in. We were hopeful that he might continue to open his eyes and interact with us as we sat keeping a vigil around the clock in his hospital room. When it was time to give other members of the family a turn, we would quietly exit the room, being careful not to disturb Dad's peaceful rest.

Glued to every slight movement, we were ready to offer food or water to Dad. The stillness of his body was eerily unfamiliar. Unsure about what to expect, we stared at the monitors and observed every change in heart rate, respiration, and blood pressure as if we would be able to will it all to stop moving in the wrong direction. In fact, every vital sign was moving in the wrong direction. We stared in disbelief, not wanting to admit to any of it. When Mom would ask what all the beeping was about, we would just give her a hug, reassuring her that all would be okay. She was not ready to let him go. Dad's heart was working hard to please her as he had done for years. Time was not on his side, and his heart was growing tired.

After that Saturday, he did not open his eyes or eat again. He stopped responding to questions about whether he would like some food. For the next few days, it was clear he was intensely focused on his entry into the afterlife. At our request, all medications were to be continued. Blood was taken each night, and sugar levels were checked twice per day. In the morning, we would study the printout of the bloodwork and focus on the smallest improvement and ignore the deteriorating ones. Wednesday morning's bloodwork report was hard to ignore. They were consistent with Dad's stillness. Clearly, his focus was on the next task. His heart was still working extremely hard, and his breaths were becoming more labored and shallower. All signs pointed to the fact that he was working hard to prepare to leave our world.

It was now Thursday morning. Hours slipped away as Dad's vital signs deteriorated, and Mom and I kept vigil. My reading of Rumi was interrupted by random thoughts, memories, and quiet sobs. I was jolted by another nurse's entrance into the dark and solemn room. She took his vitals, saying nothing, and then walked out, letting us know she was there if we needed anything at all. "Thank you" were the only words that would come out.

My mom was on one side, still holding Dad's hand and leaning on his chest, and I was on the other side, clenching my dad's hand like I had when I was a little girl. I was present physically, but mentally, I was contemplating his life over the years. Life was beautiful and cherished by him, no matter how many obstacles it presented. Determined to succeed, he never gave up trying to beat the odds. Cancer was no different.

Although he was never a fan of leaving his family, the peacefulness on his face showed his acceptance of the voyage to a better place. Perhaps overjoyed with seeing his late father or his older and younger brothers, who had both passed in recent years, gave him the strength to say goodbye to all of us. An angelic look on his face signaled that the final moments might be near.

It was just the two of us in the room with Dad. My prayer was to be with Dad until his very last breath. It was answered. Signifying the end, his shallow breaths were more deliberate and getting farther apart. Scared of what would be next, I quickly grabbed Dad's wrist, reassuring myself that his heart was still beating. Imagining him gone was so difficult. I wanted to believe this was all a nightmare and that I would soon wake up to see him smiling and telling jokes. There were so many unfinished conversations and so many stories to be told, yet it did not seem to matter. I began to speak to him in a whisper, making sure he knew I was there. "Daddy, please know I am here. Please know I love you and that you will forever be in my heart and soul. I am not ready for you to leave, yet I realize you have endured so much. You have loved your life so much, and to have it end so abruptly was not what you had planned. Your grandchildren will miss you. Your little girls, now moms themselves, are devastated. Mom is here with you and will be with you forever."

I could no longer hear Dad's shallow breaths. Mom looked over to me, with tears running down her face, still holding on to Dad's hand and crying aloud, "I feel like a piece of my heart was just ripped out of my chest." I held his wrist, hoping to detect a heartbeat. It was barely noticeable but still there. Seconds later, it was no longer palpable. As I broke into an audible moan, grieving his loss, my younger sister walked into the room, carrying the cups of coffee on a tray. One look at us and she knew he was gone. The end of a precious life had arrived. I imagined Dad being lifted to heaven, and I could almost hear his final words: "Thank you for coming."

For bonuses go to ...

When I Die

"When I die
When my coffin is being taken out
You must never think
I am missing this world

Don't shed any tears
Don't lament or
Feel sorry
I'm not falling into a monster's abyss

When you see my corpse is being carried
Don't cry for my leaving
I'm not leaving
I am arriving at eternal love

When you leave me
in the grave
Don't say goodbye
Remember a grave is
only a curtain
For the paradise behind

You'll only see me
Descending into a grave
Now watch me rise
How can there be an end
When the sun sets or
the moon goes down

www.HealthcareParachute.com

It looks like the end
It seems like a sunset
But in reality, it is a dawn
When the grave locks you up
That is when your soul is freed

Have you ever seen a seed fallen to earth
not rise with a new life
Why should you doubt the rise
Of a seed named human

Have you ever seen
A bucket lowered into a well
Coming back empty
Why lament for a soul
When it can come back
Like joseph from the well

When for the last time
you close your mouth
Your words and soul
Will belong to the world of
No place no time"

Rumi

About the Author

Shiella Dowlatshahi, a first-generation American, was born in the U.S. while her father, Dr. Bahram Dowlatshahi, was completing his medical residency. She returned to Iran with her family as a toddler for a brief period while her father continued to serve in the Shah's army and practice internal medicine. He was fortunate to return to the U.S. with the family to train further as a cardiologist. Circumstances beyond their control forced the family to stay in the U.S. after the Iranian Revolution.

Watching her father's advocacy for his patients was a source of inspiration. Not surprisingly, Shiella Dowlatshahi sought a career in health care and patient advocacy, receiving a master's degree in pain research, education, and public policy from Tufts School of Medicine in 2020. In 2014, she was also certified by Duke University as a professional in patient safety (CPPS), and received her certification in hospital patient advocacy in 2015.

Shiella has focused on advocating for the patient, both personally and professionally. Shiella has been a board member of the New England Chapter of Crohn's and Colitis Foundation since 2015, advocating on behalf of patients with these autoimmune diseases.

Shiella Dowlatshahi is a passionate patient advocate, mom, author, and an accomplished executive in the biopharmaceutical industry. During her tenure in the industry, she has been involved with the transformation of five research biopharmaceutical companies to commercial entities, successfully launching multiple novel products for rare diseases and acute care, developed to help patients achieve a better quality of care.

As a working mom, she raised her two children in Hopkinton, MA, and later relocated to Boston, where she now resides. Both of her adult children live in the Northeast.

Shiella Dowlatshahi shares lessons learned as she reflects on her family's agonizing journey and implores the reader to be an educated consumer of medicine as she tells a poignant story about her father's role as a physician, followed by his journey as a patient.

Made in the USA
Columbia, SC
19 February 2023

12700789R00078